SHANGO D'ALLEN

TRUMP HAS MY VOTE PERIOD!

I, Shango D'Allen, dedicate this book to all those that either think they are too old to start a new journey in their lives, change lanes in their life to afford new opportunities or just been stuck in apprehension and timidness. Remember even if you fail at goals if you at least chase them and participate in obtaining them I promise you opportunities will make their way to you. To do nothing will give you nothing. No matter, young or old, let's make a difference in your life and others today.

Contents

Preface

Awakening the Power of Individual Action: A Journey of
Self-Realization and Collective Impact

EDMUND BURKE once said, "Nobody makes a greater mistake than he who does nothing because he could do only a little." This quote speaks to a universal truth that resonates deeply within many of us. It touches on the struggle of feeling insignificant, the nagging thought that one person's efforts are too small to matter. For years, these thoughts plagued me, holding me back from acting on the ideas that filled my mind and soul. The belief that as one person, I could never accomplish anything significant kept me from taking even the smallest steps. But after decades of wrestling with this mindset, I finally realized that the most significant mistake is doing nothing at all. It's a realization that I know I share with many others who have felt similarly trapped by their doubts.

The journey to this realization was not easy, but it was necessary. It began with acknowledging the persistent voice within me, urging me to try, to do something, anything, rather than remain passive. That voice grew louder over time, fueled by the frustration of watching the world around me and feeling powerless to make a difference. But as the quote by Edmund Burke suggests, doing nothing because we can only do a little is the greatest mistake we can make. It is inaction, not the size of our actions, that is the true enemy of progress.

Throughout my life, I've heard a saying, one not attributed to any famous figure, yet it carries profound wisdom: "A single drop of water may seem inconsequential, but countless drops together form rivers and oceans." This saying encapsulates the power of collective action, the idea that while one person's efforts may seem small, when combined with others, they can create something vast and powerful. It's a reminder that we should not be discouraged by the magnitude of the challenges we face but instead recognize the potential of working together. Alone, we may be like drops of water, easily evaporated and forgotten. But united, we become a force to be reckoned with, capable of shaping the world around us.

For far too long, I allowed myself to be that single drop, drying up in the heat of doubt and inaction. I was tired—sick and tired, as they say—of waiting for someone else to step up and be the savior, to fix the problems that seemed too big for me to tackle alone. But the truth is, no one is coming to save us. We must save ourselves. This realization became the driving force behind my decision to write this book, a decision that marks the beginning of my journey to reclaim my sense of purpose and agency. This book is more than just words on a page; it is my declaration to the world that I will no longer allow myself to feel inadequate or powerless. It is the first step in doing my part to make a difference.

This book is also an invitation to you, the reader. It is a call to action for those who, like me, value God, family, community, state, and country. If you share these principles and are ready to take meaningful action, then join me and others who are committed to building a better society. Together, we can create a network of individuals who are willing to contribute their ideas, their time, and their resources to a collective effort aimed at making real change.

My intentions with this book are clear: to raise the necessary funds to launch a sophisticated, for-profit marketing program that will finance a new social infrastructure. This infrastructure will be designed to assist and support those who are willing to help build a better society. I firmly believe that it is time we stop relying so heavily on the government to solve our problems and start taking responsibility for our communities. By doing so, we can free up the government to focus on larger, more global issues, while we take care of our own.

It is easy to be cynical, to sit back and criticize without ever lifting a finger to help. But that kind of attitude gets us nowhere. If you find yourself in that mindset, I challenge you to look in the mirror, stare into your own eyes, and confront the truth. Ask yourself if you are truly satisfied with doing nothing, with being just another voice in the chorus of complaints. Or are you ready to be part of the solution, to take action and make a difference, no matter how small your contributions might seem at first?

This journey is not just about me; it is about all of us. It is about recognizing the power we have as individuals and as a collective. It is about understanding that while we may not be able to change the world overnight, we can start by making small changes in our own lives and in our communities. These small actions, when multiplied by many, have the potential to create a ripple effect that can lead to significant, lasting change.

So, I invite you to join me on this journey. Let us not make the mistake of doing nothing because we can only do a little. Instead, let us come together, each contributing what we can, to build something greater than ourselves. This book is the beginning of that journey, a step toward creating a movement that values action over inaction, hope over despair, and collective effort over individual isolation.

The road ahead will not be easy, but it will be worth it. Together, we can become that immense body of water, strong enough to nourish those in need or to sweep away the obstacles that stand in our way. The choice is ours to make, and I have already made mine. I hope you will join me, not just as a reader of this book, but as a fellow traveler on this path toward a better future.

Remember that the power to change the world lies within each of us. It is not about having to be rich or being a politician, but it's about not giving into limiting oneself and doing the small, consistent actions every day. It's about banding together with like minded individuals to become the force needed to enforce change. As Edmund Burke reminds us, the greatest mistake is doing nothing because we can only do a little. Let us not fall into that trap. Instead, let us commit to doing what we can, knowing that together, our efforts will add up to something truly transformative. You have the power to choose your path, and I have chosen mine. *Now, let's take action..*

Acknowledgments

*First and foremost, I offer my deepest respect and gratitude to **ALLAH** for granting life to humanity and for blessing my parents with their union that brought me into this world. I am thankful for every moment You have given me—whether it was a lesson learned, a test of my character, or an opportunity to grow through life's challenges. I am grateful for the paths You allowed me to cross with those I've come to know, love, appreciate, and enjoy wholeheartedly. As I embark on this final journey, I ask for the strength, wisdom, and guidance to live a life that pleases You. May my actions make You proud, and if it is Your will, grant me the chance to enter Heaven. I thank You deeply and sincerely for every blessing.

*To my son, **Shango**, you are a constant source of inspiration, always pushing me to strive, struggle, and fight for a legacy filled with meaning and purpose. Your existence alone fuels my desire to stay ahead, though it's no easy task because you're a force to be reckoned with. I love you with every fiber of my being. You are a blessing that keeps me sharp, motivated, and proud beyond words.

But I cannot mention you without honoring all my children, who are the light of my life. You are each a part of my heart, and

I appreciate you deeply every single day. You all give me reason to keep going, to build something greater, and to cherish this journey we are on together.

To my two beautiful grandchildren—my hearts, my joys—you are the purest blessings I could ever ask for. Your smiles, laughter, and innocence remind me of the importance of legacy and love. You two fill my soul with a joy that words can never fully capture. I am forever grateful for the love you bring into my life.

I love all of you, deeply and endlessly, with every inch of my existence.

Eminem: I want to give my deepest appreciation to Eminem for writing and performing "Lose Yourself." That song was a constant source of focus, grounding, and motivation through-out this journey. I played it over and over, and every time I needed a push, that track gave me the strength to keep moving forward. Honestly, I don't think I would've been able to write this book as quickly without it. For the record, and let it be known—regardless of his skin color, Eminem is without question one of the top 10 greatest rappers of all time. He's solidly in my personal top 5. There, I said it, and I mean it.

The essence of "**Lose Yourself**" (https://youtu.be/k6604pV6 5KY?si=fwXhqNF2vQbAJ24L) is about capturing the moment and not letting fear or doubt stand in the way. Eminem masterfully paints a picture of the pressure we face when opportunity strikes, and the importance of giving everything you've got, knowing you may never get another shot. It's about rising above failure, facing obstacles head-on, and holding onto your dreams despite the challenges.

For me, "**Lose Yourself**" stands as one of the most positively impactful rap songs ever made. Its message of resilience, perseverance, and overcoming adversity resonates deeply, making it a timeless anthem for anyone striving for greatness or battling difficult circumstances. The power of the song lies in its ability to spark action, reminding us all to seize every opportunity and never let fear hold us back. Thank you, Eminem, for being an inspiration when I needed it the most.

*My Bro and Great Friend; 8ball, who I call "*8Ball2DaMax*", I give major props and gratefulness to for not only giving me somewhere in which I could hide out from the world to get this done but from always being that positive voice helping me find my way.

*To my 2nd Ex-Wife "*Bueka*" I hold warmth and appreciation for. Although, we went our separate ways from marriage you've been a constant blessing in my life. I owe you so much because you've never let me down whenever I needed someone to be there for me regardless of what it was. You have shown me the proof that unconditional love is a real thing.

*To **Kesha**. The amount of motivation I received from you even unknowingly surmounted to a need that I will always be grateful for. Thanks.

*__Shanelle__, girl you crazy as but definitely stood in support of my accomplishment of this task. I appreciate you and although I still don't know what to call our relationship because you know I don't believe in calling anyone I had a thang with a friend I'm grateful for your honesty and support.

*__50 Cents__, well like Eminem's song that gave me that constant boost of focus because of the connection it has to my present situation, you on the other hand supplied music that gave my soul that hype to tackle everything with the aggressiveness I needed. From working out, to hustling with the truck driving to the attitude I had when I needed to say F it all I'm going to take time for myself and write this book. Your music has always been right up my alley but on this mission it's been appreciative to have it part of the pathway to my grabbing my new life.

*To my Big Sis; "__TEO__", thanks for always making sure I know that I'm special and always appreciating what I've always done for my family and loved ones. Even though they don't always let me know you do for them and that's what's up. Thank you from the deepest part of my soul.

*To __Momma P__; Paula Akins, you always stay checking on me and not only making sure I'm alright physically but alright spiritually. You are and have always been a blessing. Love you lady.

__Elon Musk__: I've been a supporter of yours since the early days of Tesla, and I've always admired how you set out to live your vision without compromising the planet. Your ability to pursue bold ideas that challenge the status quo while keeping sustainability at the forefront speaks volumes. It's always been a dream of mine to sit down with you, just to soak up some of that brilliance, and maybe one day I'll get that honor. You're one of my greatest inspirations—not because of your wealth, but because of your humility and relentless drive to find solutions that will impact humanity for generations to come. And on top of that, being a father to 12 children—now that's heroic in its own right!

Thank you for backing up Donald Trump and being a vocal and active defender of freedom of speech. Your courage in standing up for what you believe in, regardless of how controversial it may be, is truly inspiring. Keep pushing boundaries, Elon— your work is shaping the future, and we're all better for it.

@MegynKelly:
   https://youtube.com/shorts/2lXkxQy8EjE?si=pBmeo_Eu88 OHfNB6

Now this lady here gives me what I need. Megyn, your fearless approach to journalism and unwavering dedication to uncovering the truth is remarkable. You dig deep, ask the tough questions, and hold no punches, all while maintaining a level of professionalism and intelligence that sets you apart. Your ability to tackle complex issues with clarity and integrity is something I deeply respect. In a time when many shy away from controversy, you stand firm, delivering the facts with courage and insight. Thank you for being a relentless voice in media, one that continues to challenge, inform, and inspire. Keep doing what you do best—leading with strength and conviction.

@DeVoryDarkins:
   https://youtube.com/shorts/u-b1pQEZ60o?si=TReXHbCLN wsrLp44

DeVory Darkins is a young, diligent, and highly respected podcaster who brings authenticity, intention, and professionalism to the forefront. In his righteous quest to shape his strong voice and stance, he backs it up with thorough research, a keen sense of the issues, and an unwavering commitment to the truth. At a time when many avoid controversy out of fear of backlash, Darkins stands firm, reporting with integrity and conviction. Keep up the great work, young brother. We see you, and we proudly stand in support.

Patrick Bet-David @Valuetainmenthighlights:
   https://youtube.com/shorts/7QonYibNuVY?si=RBPxlWdiOY YE___bM

I look at a lot of Patrick videos on different channels and not just shorts. He has a wide array of life topics he gets heavy about and he comes from a place in which you know he has experience and been through some tough life to get where he got to. And he is the kind of interviewer that gets down to the bottom of things without having to try and show off his brain. He keeps it simple or at least will simplify it for his audience but is astute at getting what he wants from his guest. Check him out: life, politics, money, family. He speaks it all.

@*kevinoleary*:
  https://youtube.com/shorts/NIzyMzmUnYg?si=EW4y7f20A 3UQ26Tc

What I like about O'Leary is the fact he goes for the jugular all the time. He plays no games. He looks at everything from an investment angel no matter what it is. I appreciate that because to me you have to look at politics that way if you really are looking to get anything out of it. If not then you'll be fed lies and looking stupid each term.

Candace Owens:
  https://youtube.com/shorts/eta5GO5S3pU?si=WIXD8Rocqt k-vPiz

Candace, your courage, resilience, and unapologetic stance in the face of adversity are truly inspiring. You're a force of nature, never backing down from speaking the truth, no matter how uncomfortable or unpopular it may be. Your intellect, poise, and relentless pursuit of honesty have made you a beacon for those who value integrity in a world where it's often compromised. Your ability to challenge the status quo with unwavering conviction is a testament to your strength and leadership. Thank you for being a powerful voice for truth and for standing firm in your beliefs. You inspire many, including myself. Keep leading the charge.

@blackconservative2429:
https://youtube.com/shorts/___c6bjKGI80?si=Hc1RVv33Uv 75sd9j
https://youtube.com/shorts/O2lsd-1cqe0?si=5Ot3pI2uAo_b 6YxE

"This shows just how disconnected some Democrat voters are today. It's frustrating that they get upset when you say you're voting for Trump because you believe he's the better candidate to help restructure policies and strengthen the economy. Then, you hear reasons like this for voting—based on something as trivial as sharing a birthday. Come on, seriously!"

@VivekGRamaswamy:
https://youtube.com/shorts/LTqDUOGK6m8?si=ywlRMyh9 TAvJTWrv

Now I like this guy here. He's always professional, very articulate, never gets out of character or loses his cool, he has true clarity about not just the issues but the people themselves and you can't pull a fast one on him. I look forward to keeping him on my radar and seeing how he progresses.

Senator Hawley: We should call you the "Garbage Man" because you are definitely trying to take out all the trash with those hearings. You are relentless and I glad there is finally someone not willing to take a blind eye stance against corruption and ill practices in government and industry.

@TuckerCarlson:
  https://youtube.com/shorts/n8vpqx6IfAY?si=ukof7HCS9K6BBXjH

Now Tucker C is definitely one of those on the front line guys fighting the battle every chance he gets. He goes looking for the smoke wherever it may be. He's like a Marine when it comes to fighting issues and rearranging ignorance face. I learn a lot from this guy through his war like debates and he has a twist of wit too so he commands whatever crowd he faces.

Joe Rogan:
  https://youtu.be/tAJUwiAqW38?si=qj7eU8oR-4iOnGTs

Man what can I say that everyone doesn't already know. You da shit, bro. The amount of various information you put out here in the spectrum is unbelievable. You answer questions before some can formulate the question in their minds.

@docrich:
  https://youtube.com/shorts/eRQhMCSGxT0?si=c4igVuQHYLlykY9c

Now Doc-Rich has a wide range of videos he like to do reactions on but he has been going hard on bringing the public the play by play throughout this campaign and I've been grateful because I'll see something on one of his shorts that will make me go deeper into research. Good looks Bro

@*theOfficerTatum:*
   https://youtube.com/shorts/bVh06T2HrGA?si=psRv4BrdPi
dPU5Z2

"This woman didn't hold back, speaking the truth clearly. She called out how liberals are putting up signs across Chicago's urban areas to incite tension between illegal immigrants and Black residents, all as part of a plan to push Black people out of their neighborhoods and replace them with immigrants to secure more government funding. There's a lot of manipulation and injustice happening, targeting lower- to middle-class Americans, regardless of race, religion, or creed."

@*RedShortsPolitics:*
   https://youtube.com/shorts/CKatrW_9rhs?si=e4r-BP8Now
by9z-K

I like RedShortsPolitics because he sticks to what comes out the horses mouth. No trying to do his own little translation remix. His video shorts are straight politics and no interpretations. Straight from the government's voice box. Keep up the good work.

And last but never least

The 45th and hopefully the soon to be 47th President DONALD TRUMP... and I don't have to write anything about you because this entire book is dedicated to my support for you. Just make sure you be blessed and always prosperous.

Trump keeps it so 100 can't see how people can't respect that
https://youtube.com/shorts/52HIOtECfKY?si=EracEj-EedU POM2J

Respectfully Submitted By:
Shango D'Allen
trumphasmyvoteperiod2024@gmail.com

Introduction

A Call to Action for a Divided World

In today's rapidly changing world, we find ourselves more divided than ever before. Political, social, and economic divides have become deep-rooted, and many of us feel trapped in a cycle of conflict, confusion, and helplessness. At times, it may seem as though the challenges we face—be it economic disparity, social unrest, environmental degradation, or health crises—are too vast for any one person or community to solve. Our instinct, understandably, is to look toward those in power: to politicians, leaders, and government institutions, hoping that someone will step forward with the perfect solution to fix what is broken. But what if I told you that the most powerful force for change isn't found in the halls of government or in the offices of corporate elites? What if true change begins in a much more familiar place—within ourselves, our communities, and the actions we take in our everyday lives?

Throughout history, we've witnessed the failure of relying solely on governments or policies to create lasting, meaningful change. We've seen revolutions, reforms, and movements that

1

have come and gone, often leaving people disillusioned when their ideal solutions don't materialize. But what if the answer isn't about who holds the highest office, or which party is in power, but about who we are as individuals and how we come together as a collective? This book is not only a reflection of my personal beliefs, but it is also an urgent call for all of us to reclaim our power. To recognize that we, as ordinary citizens, hold the key to a brighter future—not only for ourselves but for the generations that follow.

As you read through these pages, you'll see a recurring theme: the power of the individual to affect real change. It's a message that I hold dear because I have lived it. I grew up witnessing firsthand the profound effects of political decisions on real people in real communities. I saw the impact of economic policies that neglected the working class, and I watched how entire communities were left behind because those in power didn't understand or prioritize the needs of everyday people. But I also witnessed something else—something far more inspiring. I saw the resilience and strength of ordinary people who refused to give in to despair. I saw communities come together in the face of adversity, united by a shared goal of building something better, even when the odds were stacked against them.

The solutions to our problems will never come solely from Washington, D.C. or from any government institution. It is not a matter of simply electing the "right" leader, nor is it about passing the perfect piece of legislation. While these things can certainly help, they are not the foundation upon which true, lasting change is built. That foundation is made up of you, me, and every individual who chooses to take responsibility for the future. The strength of our nation has always been in its people—ordinary men and women who refuse to give up on the promise of a better tomorrow.

We are currently living in a time of unprecedented challenges. The economic system that once provided for so many has become increasingly unstable. The healthcare system, which was supposed to protect us in times of crisis, has been exposed as flawed and in need of deep reform. Trust in our political institutions is at an all-time low, and social unrest has become a daily occurrence. From rising inflation to soaring healthcare costs, from the erosion of the middle class to the widening wealth gap, we are facing some of the toughest challenges in our nation's history. And yet, despite all of this, I remain hopeful.

Why? Because I believe in the power of ordinary people to rise up and demand something better. I believe in the strength of communities to come together and solve their own problems when given the tools and support they need. And I believe that if we work together, we can create a future that is more just, more equitable, and more prosperous for everyone—not just the privileged few.

This book is a blueprint for action. It is not just a collection of my thoughts and beliefs; it is an invitation to anyone who cares about the future of our country to step up and take an active role in shaping that future. This is not the time for passivity or for waiting on others to solve the problems we see in our communities. This is a time for action, for bold ideas, and for a commitment to doing the hard work required to bring about real change.

One of the most important lessons I've learned in my life is the value of personal accountability. I learned early on that waiting for someone else to come along and fix things is not a recipe for success. If we want something to change, we have to be willing to roll up our sleeves and make it happen ourselves. This book will take you on a journey—one that starts with understanding the role we each play in shaping society and the importance of personal accountability. It will challenge you to look at your own life and ask yourself: What am I doing to make a difference? What steps can I take to contribute to the betterment of my community, my nation, and my world?

As we progress through this book, I will share with you the lessons I've learned from my own experiences—growing up in a tough urban environment, navigating the political landscape, and ultimately coming to a place where I realized that true change starts from within. You'll hear about my political awakening, my journey through various U.S. presidencies, and how each leader—from Jimmy Carter to Donald Trump—impacted our nation in different ways. I'll share insights into the policies and leaders that shaped our history, but more importantly, I'll share my thoughts on where we need to go from here.

We will delve into the issues that affect us all—economic stability, healthcare reform, immigration, education, and more. These are not just political talking points; they are real issues that impact the lives of everyday Americans. Too often, these issues are reduced to soundbites in political debates, but the reality is far more complex. Economic policies that prioritize corporate interests over the needs of working families, healthcare systems that are broken and inaccessible to many, an education system that fails to prepare our children for the future—these are the challenges we must confront if we are serious about building a better future.

But this book is not just about diagnosing the problems. It's about offering solutions—real, practical strategies that we can use to build a more prosperous, just, and unified society. From innovative economic policies that prioritize the working class to cutting-edge technological advancements that have the potential to revolutionize entire industries, I'll lay out a vision for the future that is rooted in the belief that we can—and must—do better.

I want to be clear: this book is not a political manifesto. It is not about promoting one party over another, or about pushing a particular political agenda. It is about something far more important. It is about recognizing the power that each of us holds to shape the future. It is about understanding that, while the challenges we face may be great, the potential for positive change is even greater. And it is about inspiring you to take action—to get involved in your community, to advocate for the causes you believe in, and to be an active participant in the creation of a better world.

As we look to the future, we must recognize that we are at a critical juncture. The decisions we make today will have far-reaching consequences for generations to come. That is why we cannot afford to be passive or to rely on others to make those decisions for us. Each of us has a role to play in shaping the future, and together, we can build a society that reflects our highest values—one that is rooted in justice, fairness, and opportunity for all.

In the final chapters of this book, we'll explore what the future might hold. From the upcoming elections to the potential for new presidencies, we'll look at the political landscape and the choices that lie ahead. But more importantly, we'll focus on the future we want to create. What kind of society do we want to live in? What kind of world do we want to leave for our children and grandchildren? These are the questions that will guide us as we move forward, and the answers will shape the course of history.

This is a call to action for anyone who believes in the power of individuals to effect real change. It's for anyone who is tired of feeling helpless in the face of seemingly insurmountable challenges and who is ready to take a stand for what they believe in. It's for those who understand that true change doesn't come from the top down—it comes from the bottom up. It starts with each of us, in our own communities, taking small but meaningful steps toward a better future.

I invite you to join me on this journey. Together, we can build the kind of society we want to see—a society that is more just, more equitable, and more compassionate. The future is ours to shape, and it begins with the choices we make today. Let's make them count.

Video Links:

https://youtube.com/shorts/zcyZo_yZjXo?si=9bMnc9BEDS
V9braL

Chapter One: A Father's Love and a Mother's Struggles—Lessons from My Past

Growing up in an overcrowded, urban metropolitan environment, life was rarely easy. Crime, poverty, and broken families were so common that they became part of the everyday fabric of life. You learned early on to keep your guard up, not just because of the physical dangers but also because of the emotional walls you needed to build to protect yourself. The constant noise of the city, the pollution in the air, and the aggressive attitudes people developed to survive shaped the environment I grew up in. In such a place, survival wasn't a choice; it was a necessity. If you let your guard down, even for a moment, you could easily find yourself in trouble.

The city tested me in many ways, but it also taught me resilience. I watched people around me struggle, and many times, that struggle broke them. But for those who survived and even thrived, it was because they had learned to navigate the challenges that came with urban life. You had to know how to defend yourself physically and emotionally. You had to be smart, sharp, and always aware of your surroundings. Life in the city didn't give you the luxury of being naive.

Despite how harsh that reality could be, we found ways to make it through. In my era, we didn't have many options, but we made something out of nothing. That's what life in those environments teaches you—to be resourceful, to push through even when the odds are stacked against you, and to lean on each other when you're struggling. We were accountable to one another, and there was a sense of community that I don't see as much anymore. When you messed up, there was always someone—whether it was family, a neighbor, or an elder—who would pull you aside and set you straight. Accountability was part of the culture, not just a concept.

Faith as a Pillar of Survival

Faith played a huge role in that accountability. Religion and spirituality were at the core of everything we did. The church, the mosque, and the neighborhood gatherings were places where people didn't just go to worship; they went to find strength, to reconnect with their purpose, and to be reminded that there was something bigger than their immediate struggles. For many of us, faith wasn't just a practice; it was survival. It's what got us through the hardest days when nothing else could.

My upbringing in Islam, the discipline it required, and the

community it built around me were foundational. My parents raised me in the faith, and I remember learning how to read through Islamic teachings. The idea of seeking knowledge, not just for the sake of knowing but to better yourself and help others, was ingrained in me from a young age. However, as I got older and life became more complex, I found myself questioning whether my faith was truly mine or just a result of my upbringing.

At one point, I began to explore other religions—Christianity, Judaism, the teachings of the Israelite's, even Buddhism. I wanted to know if the truth I had been taught was universal or if I needed to find a new path. I studied these belief systems with the same intensity I had applied to learning about Islam, and what I found was a series of common threads that connected them all. Each faith spoke about the same higher power, the same principles of good and evil, and the same need for compassion, charity, and forgiveness.

It was during this exploration that I realized that my belief in Allah wasn't just because I was born into it. I truly believed in the God that created the heavens and the earth, the universe and everything in it. The teachings of Islam spoke to me in a way that nothing else did, and I understood that being Muslim wasn't about being different—it was about embracing the same God that others sought in their own ways. This understanding deepened my respect for people of all faiths. I came to believe that we are all God's creations, and it is our duty to do good by one another, regardless of our religious differences.

But with that realization came the understanding that faith

is not just about personal salvation. It's about action. It's about taking the gifts and knowledge God has given you and using them to make the world a better place. That's why I feel compelled to help others—to do more good in this world than bad, in hopes that Allah will have mercy on me when my time comes.

A Mother's Struggles and a Son's Pain

While faith was a central pillar in my life, so were the challenges within my family, particularly my relationship with my mother. My mother, despite all her struggles, was part of that larger community I grew up in. She had her battles, her demons, and she couldn't always be the mother I needed her to be. It took me years to come to terms with her choices and the impact they had on me. For so long, I felt abandoned. I couldn't understand how a mother could walk away from her child. The pain of her absence lingered in my life, shaping my sense of self-worth and pushing me down some dark paths.

For years, I was trapped in self-pity, self-destruction, and self-mutilation. The belief that my own mother didn't love me poisoned my mind. If she couldn't love me, who else ever could? That thought consumed me for a long time. I became numb, convinced that my only relief came from the pain I carried. It was during those years that I drifted into the streets, looking for something to ease the suffering. The streets were my escape, but they were also a prison.

My mother's story is a complicated one. She came from a

11

proud, Catholic background where a woman's reputation was everything. Her family believed a woman should be married, should submit to her husband, and should never appear weak. But her choices in men reflected her deep-seated insecurities. By the time she met my father, she had been through enough bad relationships that her trust in men was nearly gone.

She was married five times, twice to the worst of men, including one who treated her so poorly that no matter how many times I tried to rescue her, she always chose him over me. I watched as she spiraled deeper into toxic relationships, refusing to see the damage it was doing to her and to our family. Each time, it broke my heart a little more, knowing that she could have had a better life with my father.

But as much as I wanted to blame her, I eventually came to realize that she, too, was a victim of the pressures and expectations placed on her. She was trapped in her own cycle of fear and insecurity, unable to break free. Her love for me was real, but it was buried under layers of pain, pride, and unresolved trauma. It took me years to understand that her choices weren't a reflection of her feelings for me—they were a reflection of her own brokenness.

It wasn't until her deathbed that I finally found closure. She asked for my forgiveness, and as I cut a few dreads from her hair to keep with me, I released the pain I had carried for so long. I used to think closure was a myth, something people talked about but never truly achieved. But in that moment, I realized that closure wasn't just about moving on; it was about understanding, forgiving, and finally letting go.

My Father: The Anchor in My Life

While my relationship with my mother was complicated, my father was the one constant in my life. He never gave up on me, no matter how far I strayed. He didn't just tell me how to live a good life; he showed me through his own example. My father was a man of honor, integrity, and resilience, and he lived those values every day. Even when I was at my worst, when I was running wild and making terrible decisions, he remained steady. He taught me what it meant to be a man, not by preaching, but by showing me.

My father wasn't just a father to me—he was a father figure to many. He believed that the success of one person in the community was the success of everyone. He wasn't just there for me; he was there for anyone who needed him. That's what I came to understand about community—it's not just about being connected; it's about being responsible for each other's well-being. We rise and fall together.

He was the kind of man who would invite me to join him, no matter how many times I had disappointed him. He'd show me how to cook, how to fix things, and he'd take me along to community events where I could see him in his element, helping others and making a difference. My father was a DJ, a community man, and a figure of peace, and through him, I learned the importance of community and the power of unconditional love.

Losing My Father: The Moment That Changed Everything

13

My father's love and guidance were what ultimately brought me back from the edge. But it wasn't until I lost him that I truly understood the depth of his impact on me. I'll never forget the day I saw him walking across the street, trying to make it to court to support me as I was being taken away in a prison transport van. That was the last time I saw him alive. Months later, while I was still in prison, I got the devastating news that he had passed away from a heart attack. The shame I felt was overwhelming. I had let him down. He had always believed in me, even when I didn't believe in myself, and now he was gone. The man who had always been my anchor, the one who had guided me through my worst moments, was no longer there. The guilt and pain I felt were unlike anything I had ever experienced before.

That moment was my breaking point. It forced me to confront everything I had done wrong, everything I had run from. It was then that I vowed to live a life that would make him proud, a life that honored the man he was and the lessons he had taught me. My father had always told me that I was meant for something bigger, something more important than the life I had been living. I knew I couldn't continue down the path I was on. I had to change. I had to be better—not just for myself, but for him.

His death became the catalyst for my transformation. I made a promise to myself that I would never waste the life he had fought so hard to save. My father had given me the tools, the wisdom, and the love I needed to survive. Now, it was up to me to use them to build a future that would honor his memory.

My Journey Into the Streets: Survival at Any Cost

Before I found my way back, however, I went through some of the darkest moments of my life. After being shuffled around between family members and struggling with the pain of my mother's abandonment, I eventually found myself on the streets. I was young, angry, and looking for any way to escape the hurt that was eating away at me. The streets offered that escape, but they also came with a price.

It started innocently enough—I was just a kid hanging out with friends, trying to fit in, trying to find some sense of belonging. But it didn't take long before I was pulled into the world of hustling. It was a dangerous world, but it was one that promised quick money and respect, two things I desperately craved at the time. I thought that if I could just make enough money, if I could just prove myself to the people around me, then maybe I could numb the pain I was feeling inside.

I started running with older guys who taught me the ropes. They showed me how to hustle, how to navigate the dangers of the streets, and how to survive in a world where trust was scarce, and loyalty was everything. I learned quickly, but the deeper I got into that life, the more I realized that there was no real loyalty in the streets. Everyone was out for themselves, and betrayal was just another part of the game.

But at the time, I didn't care. I had money in my pocket, and for a while, that was enough. I would buy things for everyone— trying to fill the emptiness inside by surrounding myself with people who seemed to care about me, at least as long as I was paying. But one of the OGs I looked up to pulled me aside one day and told me something that stuck with me. He said, "You gotta stop doing that. These people got mothers and fathers to go home to. You don't. You need to take care of yourself because no one else will."

He was right. I had been using money to buy the affection and approval I thought I needed, but at the end of the day, I was still alone. My family wasn't there, and the people I was surrounding myself with didn't really care about me. They cared about what I could give them. That realization hit hard, but it didn't stop me from continuing down that path for a while longer. The streets had a hold on me, and breaking free wasn't easy.

The Breaking Point: Violence and Near-Death Experiences

The streets weren't just about hustling for money—they were about survival. And survival meant violence. I was involved in more fights than I can count, some of them life-threatening. There were times when I came face-to-face with death, and looking back, I realize how close I came to losing everything.

One of those moments happened late one night at a subway station. I was talking to a girl, minding my own business, when a group of kids from the projects approached me. One of them pulled a gun on me and told his friend to shoot. I had a reputation on the streets, so they hesitated. But the gun was still pointed at me, and I knew I had to think fast.

I had a gun on me, too, but reaching for it would have been a death sentence. The kid with the gun kept looking at me, and I could see the indecision in his eyes. I was talking, trying to keep him from pulling the trigger, trying to figure out how to get out of the situation without getting killed. I could feel the tension rising, and just when I thought I might have a chance to walk away, the other kid yelled again, telling him to shoot. He opened fire.

The bullets ripped through my jacket, and I fell off my bike. Somehow, none of them hit me directly, but it was close—too close. I remember pulling my gun out of my pants leg, ready to shoot back, but something stopped me. It was like a force held me in place, and for a few seconds, I was frozen. I don't know if it was God or something else, but in that moment, I knew I couldn't pull the trigger.

As soon as I made the decision to throw my gun into the bushes, the police showed up. They came out of nowhere, swarming the area, and I knew if I hadn't made that choice, I would have been dead or in prison for life. That moment changed me. It made me realize how fragile life is and how quickly things can spiral out of control.

Redemption: The Road to Change

The streets had their grip on me, but after that night, I started to think more deeply about my life and the choices I was making. I knew that I couldn't continue down the path I was on. My father had always told me that I was meant for something bigger, something better, and for the first time in my life, I started to believe it.

But change didn't happen overnight. It was a long, painful process of confronting my past, my mistakes, and my demons. I had to unlearn the habits and mindsets that had kept me trapped in a cycle of self-destruction for so many years. I had to let go of the anger and bitterness I felt toward my mother, toward the people who had hurt me, and toward the world that had seemed so cruel and unfair.

My father's death was the turning point, but it was the love and support of the people who believed in me—my family, my community, and my faith—that gave me the strength to move forward. I found solace in my faith, returning to the teachings of Islam that had grounded me as a child. I realized that no matter how far I had strayed, Allah's mercy was always there, waiting for me to return.

A Journey Through Faith

While my foundation in Islam was strong, there was a time when I questioned whether it was truly my faith or simply what I had inherited from my parents. As a young adult, I began to explore other religions, seeking answers and understanding beyond what I had known. I delved into Christianity, Judaism, the teachings of the Israelite's, Buddhism, and even less structured spiritual practices. I wanted to know if there was something else out there for me, something that might explain the things I had gone through.

But the more I studied, the more I realized that all these faiths shared the same core beliefs. They all spoke of compassion, forgiveness, charity, and the existence of a higher power. What I found wasn't a new religion, but a reaffirmation of my belief in Allah, the Creator of the universe, the heavens, and everything in between. I came to understand that being Muslim wasn't about being different—it was about following the same God that so many others worship in their own way.

This realization didn't just deepen my connection to Islam—it also gave me a profound respect for people of all faiths. I came to believe that we are all creations of the Almighty, and our duty is to do good by one another. We may have different ways of expressing our faith, but at the end of the day, we are all part of the same creation. That understanding drives me to help others, to make the world a better place in whatever way I can.

I don't believe in judging others for their beliefs or their struggles. Instead, I believe in compassion, in doing more good than harm, and in hoping that when my time comes, Allah will have mercy on me for the good I've done. That's why I must take this journey to help others because I believe that's what life is about. You have to do more good in this world than bad if you want to have a chance at redemption.

Moving Forward: A Life of Purpose

Today, I live with purpose. I know that my past doesn't define me, but it has shaped me into the man I am today. The pain I went through, the struggles I faced, and the mistakes I made all serve as reminders of how far I've come. I've learned that life isn't about being perfect—it's about constantly striving to be better, to learn from your experiences, and to use those lessons to lift others up.

My father's love and my mother's struggles taught me resilience, compassion, and the importance of family. My time in the streets taught me survival and the value of community. And my journey through faith has given me the strength to keep moving forward, no matter what challenges come my way.

I now live my life with a sense of direction and intent that I never had before. Every step I take is driven by a desire to do better, not just for myself, but for the people around me. I've come to understand that success isn't measured by the things you accumulate or the status you achieve; it's measured by the positive impact you have on others. The legacy you leave behind is built on the lives you've touched and the good you've put into the world.

For me, this realization came not just from my experiences on the streets, but from the lessons my father imparted to me. He always believed that success wasn't just about personal gain—it was about lifting others as you rise. His life was a testament to that belief. Even though he was just one man, his influence extended far beyond his immediate circle. He helped anyone who needed it, never asking for anything in return. He lived a life of service, and that's the path I've chosen to follow.

It wasn't easy getting to this point. There were many times

when I wanted to give up, when the weight of my past seemed too heavy to bear. But each time I found myself on the brink, something would pull me back. Whether it was the memory of my father's faith in me or the understanding that Allah's mercy is always available for those who seek it, I knew I couldn't give in to despair. I had to keep moving forward.

And that's what I've done. Every day, I wake up with a renewed sense of purpose. I strive to do good in whatever way I can, whether it's by helping someone in need, offering words of encouragement, or simply living my life as an example for others to follow. I believe that we all have a responsibility to make the world a better place, even in small ways. If we all do our part, the collective impact can be immense.

The Responsibility of Leadership

As I've grown older, I've come to realize that leadership isn't about having power or authority—it's about taking responsibility. True leadership means being willing to stand up for what's right, even when it's difficult. It means being there for people when they need you most and guiding them toward a better path, just as my father did for me.

I've also learned that leadership comes with its own set of challenges. It requires humility, patience, and a deep understanding of the people you're leading. You have to be able to see things from their perspective, to understand their struggles, and to find ways to help them overcome those obstacles. It's not about telling people what to do—it's about showing them the way through your own actions.

This understanding of leadership has shaped how I approach everything in my life. Whether I'm working on a community project, mentoring someone who's going through a tough time, or simply being there for my family, I always try to lead by example. I've learned that people are more likely to follow your lead if they see you living the values you preach. Integrity, honesty, and compassion—those are the qualities that define a true leader.

Giving Back: My Commitment to the Community

One of the most important lessons I've learned in life is that you can't rise alone. The people who helped me along the way—my father, my community, even those who tried to steer me away from the streets—played a critical role in my journey. Without them, I wouldn't be where I am today. And now that I'm in a position to help others, I feel a deep sense of responsibility to give back.

I've made it my mission to support those who are struggling, whether they're facing poverty, addiction, or simply feeling lost in the world. I know what it's like to feel abandoned, to feel like there's no way out, and I want to be there for people who are going through that same darkness. I believe that everyone deserves a second chance, and I'm committed to helping people find their way back, just as others helped me.

One of the ways I give back is by working with at-risk youth. I see so much of myself in them—the same anger, the same pain, the same desire to escape. But I also see their potential, just as my father saw mine. I work with them to help them understand that their lives don't have to follow the path they're on. There's always a way out, always a better future waiting for them if they're willing to put in the work.

I've also made it a point to support people in my community who are struggling with addiction. Having battled my own demons, I understand how difficult it is to break free from the grip of drugs and alcohol. But I also know that recovery is possible, and I want to be a source of hope for those who are fighting that battle. Through mentorship, support groups, and simply being there to listen, I do what I can to help people regain control of their lives.

The Importance of Family

Through everything I've been through, one thing has remained constant: the importance of family. My relationship with my family has had its ups and downs, but in the end, they are the people who have shaped me into the person I am today. My father, with his unwavering love and support, was the foundation of my life. Even in death, his influence continues to guide me.

My mother, despite her struggles and the pain she caused me, taught me valuable lessons as well. Her life showed me the importance of forgiveness, of understanding that people are flawed, and of letting go of resentment. If I had held onto the

23

anger I felt toward her, I would have been consumed by it. But by finding closure, by forgiving her for the mistakes she made, I was able to move forward with my life.

Family isn't just about blood—it's about the people who stand by you through thick and thin. It's about the community you build around yourself, the people who lift you up when you're down and celebrate with you when you succeed. I've been blessed to have an extended family of friends, mentors, and community members who have supported me throughout my life. They are just as much a part of my family as my blood relatives, and I am forever grateful for the role they've played in my journey.

Conclusion: A New Chapter in My Life

As I write these words, I'm filled with a sense of gratitude for the life I've lived and the lessons I've learned. My journey has been far from easy, but every hardship I've faced has taught me something valuable. I've learned that resilience comes from within, that faith can guide you through even the darkest of times, and that redemption is always possible if you're willing to work for it.

I've also come to understand that life is about balance. You can't avoid pain and struggle, but you can choose how you respond to them. You can let them break you, or you can use them as fuel to push yourself toward something greater. I've chosen the latter, and I'm committed to living a life that honors the people who have helped me along the way.

This chapter of my life is about giving back, about using the knowledge and experience I've gained to help others find their way. I believe that we all have a responsibility to make the world a better place, and I'm determined to do my part. Whether it's through community work, mentorship, or simply being a good example for others to follow, I will continue to strive to make a positive impact in the lives of those around me.

And as I move forward, I carry the lessons of my past with me. I carry my father's love, my mother's struggles, the trials of the streets, and the teachings of my faith. They are all a part of me, and they all drive me to be the best version of myself.

This is just the beginning of my story. There's so much more to do, so many more lives to touch, and I'm ready for whatever challenges lie ahead. With faith in my heart and a commitment to doing good, I'm stepping into the future with purpose, ready to continue this journey of redemption, growth, and service.

Chapter Two: The Role of Community and Personal Responsibility

Being raised in Boston's urban landscape, I saw firsthand the complicated, often fragile relationship between the individual and the community. In the neighborhood where I lived, the sense of community wasn't just a pleasant ideal—it was a lifeline. Families leaned on each other, children were disciplined and guided by neighbors, and everyone played a role in keeping things in check. Yet, alongside that sense of unity was a stark contrast: a deep divide between those who had "made it" and those who struggled to get by. It wasn't unusual to see politicians, doctors, and lawyers sharing the same streets with drug dealers, gang members, and addicts. Boston's neighborhood was a melting pot of success stories and broken lives, each struggling to coexist in a space that was both uplifting and dangerous.

The tension in those streets taught me a critical lesson: no matter your background or status, personal responsibility and community engagement go hand in hand. It doesn't matter if you're a politician with a law degree or a teenager trying to survive the temptations of street life. The choices we make, and the way we interact with our neighbors, shape not just our own futures but the future of the entire community. But somewhere along the way, the belief in collective responsibility began to fade. We've grown more isolated, more focused on individual success at the expense of the community's well-being, and in doing so, we've weakened the very foundation of what makes a neighborhood thrive.

In this chapter, I want to explore the essential role of personal responsibility and community engagement in shaping a better society. While government policies can provide a framework for success, true change comes from the ground up. It comes from individuals recognizing their responsibility to themselves and their neighbors, and from communities banding together to lift each other up.

The Power of Accountability

Personal responsibility was a concept ingrained in me from a young age. In our neighborhood, if you did something wrong, you didn't just hear it from your parents—you heard it from the neighbors, too. There was an unspoken understanding that everyone played a part in raising the next generation. If you acted out on the street, someone's mother, uncle, or grand-parent would pull you aside and let you know you were out of line. And when you got home, you could bet that your parents would reinforce that lesson. This wasn't about punishment for punishment's sake. It was about accountability, about teaching you that your actions had consequences, not just for yourself but for those around you.

Back then, we didn't have the luxury of turning a blind eye to bad behavior. Our community was struggling under the weight of poverty, crime, and addiction. The crack epidemic was hitting hard, and the streets were a battleground for survival. We couldn't afford to let anyone slip through the cracks, because one person's downfall could easily lead to more chaos for everyone. The community had to act as a unit, protecting its own while holding each other accountable.

This sense of collective responsibility is something that I feel has been lost in many communities today. People are more focused on individual success, on building their own lives, and they've forgotten that the strength of a community is in its unity. We've become isolated, disconnected from our neighbors, and that disconnect allows problems to fester unchecked. When people stop caring about what happens next door, the entire neighborhood suffers.[1]

I remember being approached by some of the more successful people in my neighborhood—politicians, government workers, and even a few local celebrities. They asked me to talk to the younger kids, to help steer them away from the streets. They knew I had the respect of the youth, that I was someone they would listen to. But I always pushed back, saying, "How can I tell them to stay off the streets when I'm still out there myself?" It felt hypocritical, and I couldn't preach something I wasn't

---

[1] Testing

living.

But I didn't stop at just saying no. I challenged those same politicians and community leaders to be open about their own pasts. I knew they hadn't always been sitting in those offices or driving their nice cars. They had come from the same streets, faced the same struggles. They had hustled, made their mistakes, and eventually found a way out. I told them if they really wanted to make a difference, they had to be honest about where they came from. They needed to show these kids that change was possible because they themselves had changed.

But they refused. They didn't want to expose their pasts, didn't want to open themselves up to judgment. It was easier to give a speech, to tell me to fix the problem, than to stand in front of these kids and say, "I was where you are, and this is how I got out." And that's the tragedy of it. You can't complain about the problems in your community if you're not willing to step up and be part of the solution. We need more leaders who are willing to share their stories, to mentor the next generation, to guide them out of the darkness. Because if we don't help those struggling today, they could be the ones who cause harm tomorrow. That's the reality.

The Erosion of Community Support

As I look at the world today, I see how much has changed since my time growing up in Boston. The sense of community that once held neighborhoods together is fading. People have become more isolated, more focused on their individual lives and less concerned about what's happening next door. We've created a culture where success is measured by how far we can distance ourselves from the struggles of our neighbors. But that mindset is dangerous. When we lose our sense of collective responsibility, we weaken the very fabric of our society.

This erosion of community support is visible in everything from the rise in crime to the breakdown of family structures. When people no longer feel connected to their neighbors, when they no longer feel accountable for the well-being of others, it creates a vacuum. And in that vacuum, the worst elements of society—crime, addiction, violence—are allowed to grow unchecked. The strength of a community lies in its ability to come together in times of crisis, to protect one another, to hold each other accountable. When that unity is lost, the community begins to crumble.

We see this reflected in the streets today. The gangs that once operated under a certain code, where elders still had some level of control, have given way to a more chaotic, violent landscape. In the absence of strong community leadership, young men and women are left to fend for themselves, often turning to the streets for the sense of belonging they can't find anywhere else. The sense of family that the streets offer is a powerful pull, especially for those who come from broken homes or who have been abandoned by their families.

But the streets don't offer real love or loyalty. They offer a dangerous illusion—a false sense of security that can be taken away at any moment. The only way to break that cycle is by rebuilding the sense of community that once existed. We need to create spaces where young people feel valued, where they are held accountable but also supported, where they can see a future beyond the violence and chaos of the streets.

Personal Responsibility: The Foundation of Change

At the heart of this issue is personal responsibility. As individuals, we have a duty to take control of our own lives and to make choices that not only benefit ourselves but also contribute to the well-being of those around us. Personal responsibility doesn't mean pulling yourself up by your bootstraps while ignoring the struggles of others. It means recognizing that your actions have consequences and that those consequences ripple out to affect your family, your neighbors, and your community.

We all have a role to play in creating a better future. It's not enough to point fingers at the government or blame external factors for the problems we face. Change starts with us— with the decisions we make every day. Are we helping our neighbors, or are we turning a blind eye to their struggles? Are we mentoring the next generation, or are we leaving them to fend for themselves in a world that's stacked against them?

It's easy to feel powerless in the face of the world's problems. It's easy to think that one person can't make a difference. But that's a lie. Every act of kindness, every moment of accountability, every time we reach out to help someone else, we are making a difference. The small actions we take today have the power to create a ripple effect that can change the

31

world tomorrow.

The Role of Government: Support, Not Solution

That's not to say that government doesn't have a role to play. It absolutely does. Government policies can provide the framework for success, offering resources and opportunities for those who need them most. But government cannot replace the power of community, nor can it instill the sense of personal responsibility that's necessary for real change.

I've often said that the government should be there to support the efforts of individuals and communities, not to replace them. When we become too dependent on the government to solve our problems, we lose the sense of agency that drives personal responsibility. We start to believe that it's someone else's job to fix the problems we see in the world, and that mentality leads to complacency. It leads to a society where people stop caring about their neighbors because they assume the government will take care of it.

But the truth is, no government program, no matter how well-designed, can replace the impact of a strong, engaged community. No government official can mentor a child in the same way a neighbor can. No policy can instill the values of accountability and responsibility in the same way a family or community can. Government can help, but it cannot do it all.

A Call to Action

As I reflect on the lessons I've learned throughout my life, one thing becomes clear: we are all responsible for the future we want to create. It's not enough to hope that someone else will step in and fix things. We must be the ones to take action, to be part of the solution. Every small effort counts, whether it's guiding a young person down the right path, helping a neighbor in need, or simply making better choices for ourselves and our families. The future of our communities, our neighborhoods, and ultimately our nation, depends on each of us stepping up and doing our part.

Throughout my journey, I've seen the difference personal responsibility and community involvement can make. I've witnessed the destruction that can happen when those values are abandoned, and I've seen the incredible power of collective action when people come together for a common purpose. It's easy to feel overwhelmed by the problems we face, but we can't afford to let fear or frustration paralyze us. Every generation has its challenges, but every generation also has its leaders— those who are willing to stand up and take charge.

The truth is, none of us can do it alone. That's why community is so important. It's not about pointing fingers or waiting for someone else to make the first move. It's about each of us taking responsibility for our own actions, while also working together to lift up those around us. Whether you're a parent raising children, a teacher shaping young minds, a business owner providing jobs, or simply a neighbor who cares, you have a role to play in shaping the future.

If we want to see real, lasting change, we need to foster a culture where people care about more than just themselves. We need to revive the idea that we are all interconnected—that my success is tied to your success, and that when one of us falls, we all feel the impact. This doesn't mean sacrificing personal goals or ambitions, but rather, recognizing that in order to thrive, we need strong communities where everyone has a chance to succeed.

That's why I'm calling on all of us to look around, to see the people in our neighborhoods, in our workplaces, and in our cities who need help. Don't wait for someone else to take the lead. Be the one who steps up, who makes a difference, even if it's in a small way. You might be surprised by how much of an impact you can have, how your actions can inspire others to do the same.

We need to move away from a mindset of isolation and division and toward one of unity and support. It's time to stop thinking of success as an individual achievement and start seeing it as a collective effort. We rise together, or we fall together. That's the truth of it.

The Importance of Mentorship

One of the most powerful ways we can create change is through mentorship. When I think about the people who influenced me the most, it wasn't the politicians or celebrities; it was the everyday people who took the time to guide me, to show me a different way. It was my father, my neighbors, and the community leaders who cared enough to step in when I was heading down the wrong path. They didn't have to do it, but they chose to because they understood that the success of the community depended on the success of its young people.

We need more of that today. We need more people who are willing to mentor the next generation, to show them that there is more to life than what the streets offer. It's not about preaching or judging; it's about being present, about offering guidance and support. Sometimes all it takes is one person to believe in you, to see your potential, to help you unlock it.

If you've made it out of a tough situation, if you've found success despite the odds, it's your responsibility to reach back and help someone else do the same. Don't keep your knowledge or experience to yourself. Share it. Use it to lift someone else up. That's how we create lasting change—by investing in the people around us, by showing them that they, too, can succeed.

Mentorship isn't always about grand gestures or elaborate programs. Sometimes it's as simple as having a conversation, listening to someone who needs guidance, or showing them that there is another way forward. It's about giving your time and attention to those who may not have anyone else to turn to. I've seen firsthand how powerful mentorship can be in transforming lives, and I believe it is one of the most effective tools we have for creating real, lasting change.

The Role of Elders and Leaders in the Community

In the neighborhood where I grew up, the elders played a

significant role in shaping the lives of young people. They weren't just our parents and grandparents; they were our guides, our protectors, and our teachers. They knew the struggles we faced, and they knew the streets just as well as we did. But they also knew what it meant to live with integrity, to take responsibility for their actions, and to look out for others.

In today's world, the role of elders and community leaders has diminished in many places. Too many people are afraid to speak up, afraid to offer guidance for fear of being criticized or ignored. But our communities need these voices more than ever. The wisdom of those who have lived through hardship, who have made mistakes and learned from them, is invaluable to the next generation.

As elders and leaders, we have a responsibility to pass on what we've learned. We have to be willing to share our stories, to be honest about our failures, and to offer guidance to those who are struggling. It's not about preaching or judging—it's about showing up and being there when it matters most. Just like the elders in my neighborhood did for me, we must step up and take on that role for the next generation.

We also need to recognize that leadership isn't just about titles or positions of power. Real leadership comes from the heart. It's about doing what's right, even when it's hard. It's about standing up for what you believe in and being willing to make sacrifices for the greater good. Whether you're an elder, a parent, a teacher, or simply someone who cares about your community, you have the ability to lead by example.

The Connection Between Personal Responsibility and National Change

As I think about the role of personal responsibility in shaping communities, I can't help but reflect on the broader implications for our nation. The problems we face as a country— economic inequality, crime, addiction, and social division— are, in many ways, the same problems that plague individual communities. And just as change in a community starts with personal responsibility, so too does change at the national level.

It's easy to look at the problems in our country and feel overwhelmed. The challenges we face are massive, and they won't be solved overnight. But if we each take responsibility for our own actions, if we work to strengthen our communities and support those around us, we can begin to create the kind of change we want to see on a larger scale.

The government has a role to play, but it can't do everything. Real change comes from the ground up, from individuals and communities coming together to tackle the issues they face. If we want to see our country move in the right direction, we have to start by taking responsibility for our own lives and by investing in the well-being of our neighbors.

I've often thought about how the lessons I learned in my neighborhood could be applied on a national scale. Just as we had to hold each other accountable in our community, we need to hold each other accountable as a country. We need to recognize that the success of our nation is tied to the success of its people, and that means looking out for one another, supporting one another, and taking responsibility for the choices we make.

The Impact of Personal Responsibility on Future Generations

One of the most important reasons we must embrace personal responsibility and community involvement is for the sake of future generations. The choices we make today will shape the world our children and grandchildren inherit. If we want to leave them a better world, we have to start by making better choices for ourselves.

The values of personal responsibility, accountability, and community engagement are not just for our benefit—they are the foundation upon which future generations will build their lives. When we model these values for our children, we give them the tools they need to succeed. We show them that success is not just about individual achievement, but about contributing to the greater good.

I believe that one of the most important things we can do for future generations is to invest in their success. That means providing them with the education, mentorship, and support they need to thrive. It also means holding them accountable, teaching them the importance of responsibility, and showing them that their actions have consequences.

We can't afford to ignore the impact our choices have on future generations. If we fail to take responsibility for our own lives, if we fail to invest in our communities, we are setting the stage for future failure. But if we embrace the values of personal responsibility and community involvement, we can create a brighter future for our children and grandchildren.

Moving Forward Together

As I reflect on the lessons I've learned throughout my life, I am filled with a sense of hope. Yes, the challenges we face are great, but I believe that we have the power to overcome them. If we come together as a community, if we take responsibility for our own actions and for the well-being of those around us, we can create the kind of world we want to live in.

I refuse to believe that we are too far gone, that the problems we face are insurmountable. I refuse to accept that the violence, poverty, and division that plague our communities are inevitable. We have the power to change our circumstances, but it requires effort. It requires all of us to step up, to be leaders in our own right, and to be the ones who make a difference.

The future is unwritten. It's up to us to decide what kind of world we want to live in. Will we continue to drift apart, to focus only on ourselves, or will we come together to build a better future?

———

RESEARCH

Data and Statistics

Mentorship and Its Impact on Youth

Mentorship is one of the most powerful tools we have to shape the future of our youth. According to research from The National Mentoring Partnership, young people with mentors are **55% more likely to enroll in college** compared to those who don't have a mentor. This influence goes beyond academic success—mentored youth are also **78% more likely to volunteer regularly**, fostering a sense of social responsibility that extends into adulthood. In communities where young people face economic and social challenges, mentorship offers not just guidance but hope for a better future.

Additionally, youth with mentors are shown to engage in healthier behaviors. Studies indicate that mentored youth are **46% less likely to start using drugs** and **27% less likely to start drinking alcohol** than their peers without mentors. The role of a mentor isn't just about academic guidance—it's about helping young people make better life choices.

The power of mentorship extends to future employment, as well. The Bridgespan Group reports that youth who have mentors are more likely to find gainful employment and secure better-paying jobs. This is particularly critical in underprivileged communities, where access to career guidance is limited. The right mentor can open doors that once seemed out of reach, providing a pathway to a stable and successful career.

The Role of Community Support in Reducing Crime

Strong communities are vital in preventing crime. A 2019 study published in Social Science Research demonstrated that communities with strong social ties and high levels of neighborhood cohesion have **40% lower violent crime rates** than communities where people feel isolated and disconnected. Social capital—the network of relationships within a community—plays a crucial role in crime prevention. When people know their neighbors, look out for one another, and take pride in their community, they create a safer, more supportive environment.

Similarly, The U.S. Department of Justice found that community policing strategies, where law enforcement officers engage directly with residents to build trust and cooperation, have been able to **reduce crime rates by as much as 30%**. These efforts show that when a community is invested in its own safety and well-being, the benefits extend to everyone.

Programs like Neighborhood Watch have also proven effective in reducing crime. According to the Bureau of Justice Statistics, neighborhoods with **active Neighborhood Watch programs have been able to reduce burglaries by 16-26%**. These programs rely on the participation and vigilance of ordinary citizens, demonstrating the power of collective responsibility in keeping crime at bay.

Family Structure and Personal Responsibility

The connection between family structure and personal responsibility is profound. Children raised in two-parent households are more likely to succeed academically and in life. Data from the U.S. Census Bureau shows that children in two-parent homes are **75% more likely to graduate from high school and attend college** than those raised in single-parent homes. This underscores the critical role that family support plays in shaping future success.

Furthermore, children who grow up without a father or an engaged male role model face significant challenges. The National Fatherhood Initiative reports that children from fatherless homes are more than twice as likely to drop out of school and **70% more likely to engage in criminal behavior.** Fathers and father figures provide guidance, discipline, and emotional support that are essential to a child's development, helping them make better life choices and avoid the pitfalls of delinquency.

The Influence of Government and Social Programs

Government assistance programs play a critical role in supporting vulnerable populations, but long-term reliance on these programs can lead to dependency and stagnation. The Center on Budget and Policy Priorities found that in 2020, social safety net programs like SNAP and the Earned Income Tax Credit (EITC) lifted nearly 11 million Americans out of poverty. These programs provide much-needed relief to families struggling to make ends meet.

However, there is a downside to prolonged dependency. A study from the Heritage Foundation found that individuals who remain on welfare for extended periods, without receiving job training or employment opportunities, **are 30% more likely to remain on assistance long-term.** This creates a cycle of dependency that can trap families in poverty. It highlights the need for welfare programs that not only provide immediate relief but also offer pathways to self-sufficiency through job placement and skills development.

The Impact of Social Isolation on Community Health

Social isolation has a profound impact not only on individuals but also on communities as a whole. According to the American Psychological Association, **social isolation increases the risk of premature death by 50%**, a rate comparable to risks associated with smoking and obesity. In communities where people feel disconnected from one another, mental health declines, and with it, the overall health of the neighborhood.

Furthermore, a study from the University of Chicago showed that socially isolated individuals are twice as likely to commit violent crimes as those with strong social connections. The lack of social ties fosters a sense of alienation and frustration, which can manifest as destructive behaviors. This underscores the importance of building strong social networks within communities, where people feel connected, valued, and supported.

43

Educational Outcomes and Community Engagement

Education is the cornerstone of personal success, and strong community support plays a crucial role in fostering academic achievement. The Coalition for Community Schools reports that students who attend community schools—where academic, health, and social services are integrated—**are 10% more likely to graduate than those in traditional schools**. Community schools provide a holistic approach to education, recognizing that students' academic success is tied to their overall well-being.

After-school programs also have a significant impact on student achievement. The After-school Alliance found that students who participate in after-school programs are **30% more likely to improve in reading and math** and **60% less likely to drop out of school** than those who do not have access to such programs. After-school programs provide a safe, structured environment where students can continue learning and receive mentorship, reducing their likelihood of engaging in risky behaviors.

The Economic Impact of Strong Communities

Strong communities not only foster personal growth but also contribute to economic prosperity. A Harvard University study found that children raised in neighborhoods with high social capital—where people are actively engaged with one another and invested in each other's success—**are 20% more likely to achieve upward economic mobility**. Social connections

44

provide opportunities for mentorship, networking, and access to resources that can lift individuals and families out of poverty.

Volunteerism also has a significant economic impact. According to the Corporation for National and Community Service, volunteer efforts contributed an estimated $167 billion to the U.S. economy in 2018. Communities with high rates of volunteerism tend to have better economic outcomes, lower crime rates, and a higher quality of life. This shows that when people invest their time and energy into helping their communities, everyone benefits.

The Effectiveness of Youth Programs in Reducing Crime

Youth programs play a vital role in keeping young people off the streets and reducing crime. A 2019 study published in Youth & Society found that youth who participate in organized sports are **70% less likely to engage in criminal activities** compared to those who don't. Organized sports provide structure, discipline, and a sense of belonging—qualities that help deter youth from turning to the streets.

Additionally, **summer employment programs for young people** have been shown to significantly reduce crime rates. Research from the National Bureau of Economic Research **found that these programs reduced violent crime arrests by 43%** in the year following participation. Giving youth the opportunity to work, earn money, and develop skills not only keeps them out of trouble but also sets them on a path toward a more successful future.

If we come together as a community, armed with the kind of data and understanding this information provides, we have the power to transform not only our current circumstances but also the future for our children. Statistics like these highlight the importance of mentorship, community involvement, personal responsibility, and social accountability. When we recognize the direct impact that our collective actions—or inaction's— have on our neighborhoods, we can take steps toward fostering environments that offer opportunity, support, and security for all.

Imagine if we used these insights to prioritize community pro- grams that focus on mentoring youth and providing them with a sense of belonging. By investing in after-school programs, summer employment opportunities, and youth sports, we can reduce crime and give young people the tools they need to build successful lives. We know from the data that mentorship and strong social networks are key in preventing delinquency and setting young people on a path toward success. It's within our power to create these opportunities by supporting and organizing these kinds of initiatives within our communities.

The ripple effect of coming together as a community to support one another goes beyond just our immediate surroundings. When we mentor a child, support a struggling family, or strengthen the social fabric of our neighborhoods, we're not only improving the lives of those individuals, we're building a foundation for future generations. Our children will inherit the world we create today, and by working together, we can ensure they grow up in safer, more supportive, and more prosperous communities. Investing in each other now means a brighter, more connected future for all of us.

I am hopeful because with optimism, positivity, action, sup-port, unity, and deliberate intention, I truly believe progress, growth, and change are within reach. Whether you prove me right or wrong, the outcome depends on the effort we are willing to invest to discover the truth.

Chapter Three: Political Awakening—My Journey into Politics

By the time I was 17, I had already begun to question the political landscape that surrounded me. Growing up in Boston, I saw how people around me adhered to political identities without much thought, especially in my community where being a Democrat was the default. In my neighborhood and even in my family, it was assumed that everyone supported the Democratic Party. That assumption seemed to be woven into the very fabric of our lives. You were Black, you were working class, and you were a Democrat. It was just the way things were.

Yet, something about that never sat right with me. I couldn't put my finger on it at first, but I knew that I couldn't follow along blindly. I wasn't the type of person to simply accept what was being handed to me without question. Even at a young age, I had a sense of independence in thought and action. I didn't want to follow a political party just because that's what everyone else around me was doing.

As I started to think more critically about politics, I realized that I wasn't impressed by what I was seeing or hearing from the Democrats. It felt like a lot of empty promises and recycled rhetoric. They claimed to be the party that cared about minorities, about the working class, about lifting people up. But when I looked around at my community, I didn't see much evidence of that. The poverty was still there. The crime was still there. The lack of opportunity was still there. If the Democrats were supposed to be helping us, why wasn't our situation improving?

I wasn't content to just accept what I was told. So, I began to do my own research. I started reading books, studying political history, and listening to different perspectives. Before my 18th birthday, I had never made a firm decision about where I stood politically. I wanted to keep my mind open and not be boxed into any specific ideology just because it was expected of me. As I dug deeper into the history of the Democratic Party, what I found only strengthened my resolve to distance myself from them.

Uncovering the Historical Roots

One of the most significant revelations for me was learning about the Democratic Party's historical role in perpetuating slavery and racism in America. Growing up, we weren't taught much about the complex history of political parties in school. It was easy to get the impression that the Democrats had always been the champions of civil rights and equality. But when I started to dig into the history for myself, I discovered the

49

darker side of the party's legacy.

The Democratic Party, particularly in the South, had been the party of slave owners. Southern Democrats fought tooth and nail to keep Black people in chains, and after the Civil War, when slavery was officially abolished, they didn't stop fighting. Instead, they found new ways to maintain control through segregation, voter suppression, and violence. Jim Crow laws, lynching, and racial terrorism were all part of the Southern Democratic playbook.

Even as I was learning about this history, I could see the remnants of it still alive in my own community. Though the physical chains of slavery had been broken, the psychological and economic chains were still very much in place. And while the Democrats had rebranded themselves as the party of progress and equality, I couldn't help but feel like it was just another manipulation—an attempt to control us in a more subtle, insidious way.

I realized that the Democratic Party had historically used fear and dependence to maintain power. They made Black and Brown communities feel as though they had no other choice but to support them. If you didn't vote Democrat, you were labeled as a traitor to your race, an outsider, someone who didn't care about your people. But I wasn't going to let fear or manipulation dictate my political beliefs.

The Southern Legacy and Its Northern Migration

One of the most important insights I gained during this time of self-reflection was understanding how the political dynamics of the South had influenced Black communities in the North. After the Civil War, many Black families moved north in search of better opportunities, escaping the overt racism and violence of the South. But they didn't leave behind the political culture they had grown up with. In the South, aligning with the Democratic Party had been, for many, a matter of survival. It was the only way to get a job, to avoid the terror of groups like the Ku Klux Klan, and to maintain some semblance of security.

As these families migrated to northern cities like Boston, Chicago, and New York, they brought with them the same mindset. They passed it down to their children, and before long, it became ingrained in the community that to be Black meant to be a Democrat. No one questioned it because it was what their parents and grandparents had done. But to me, it felt like we were being manipulated, like we were being told that we had no other options.

The Republican Roots of Black America

As I continued my research, I started to realize that the idea of Black people being natural allies of the Democratic Party was a relatively recent development. Historically, it was the Republican Party that had been the party of emancipation and civil rights. Abraham Lincoln, the first Republican president, had been the one to sign the Emancipation Proclamation, freeing millions of slaves. In the years following the Civil War, many Black Americans aligned themselves with the Republican

Party because it represented freedom, opportunity, and the right to chart their own course.

But somewhere along the way, that history got twisted. Black Americans, who had once been loyal Republicans, began to shift toward the Democratic Party during the New Deal era and later during the civil rights movement. While there were legitimate reasons for that shift, I also saw it as part of a broader manipulation. The Democrats had figured out that if they could offer just enough to make Black people believe they were on their side, they could secure their votes for generations to come. And it worked. But I wasn't going to let that history be forgotten. I wasn't going to let the manipulation of the past and the present dictate my political beliefs.

My Father's Influence

Throughout this process of political discovery, my father played an important role in shaping my thinking. He was a man of great intellect and curiosity, someone who believed in the importance of being politically informed. My father never pushed his own beliefs on me, but he encouraged me to think critically, to do my own research, and to come to my own conclusions. He was a Syracuse graduate, a brilliant computer programmer who had worked on some of the first IBM PCs, but he was also much more than that.

He was a chef who taught me the importance of nourishing both the body and the soul. He was a jazz and blues DJ who loved music and believed in its power to bring people together. He was a devout Muslim who lived a life of peace and compassion. And he was a man who cared deeply about community and family. He saw politics as something that directly affected our lives, and he wanted me to understand that too.

My father would often involve me in conversations with his friends, who were all intellectuals and thinkers in their own right. They debated everything—politics, culture, religion, and society. Those discussions were invaluable to me as I navigated my own political awakening. They taught me that politics wasn't just about choosing a party—it was about understanding the impact that government and policy had on real people's lives.

A Defining Encounter at Dudley Station

One of the most pivotal moments in my political journey came during an encounter at Dudley Station. I was 18 at the time, still on the fence about where I stood politically. I had been leaning toward being an Independent, feeling disillusioned with both major political parties. I wasn't ready to commit to either side because I didn't feel like either one truly represented my values.

Then, I met a woman at Dudley Station who changed my perspective. She wasn't there to talk to me about religion or spirituality, as I had initially assumed. Instead, she wanted to talk to me about politics and government. The way she broke it down was unlike anything I had heard before. She explained politics as a game—one where you had to understand the rules and the players, or you would always end up losing.

Her words resonated with me deeply because I had already seen the truth of that in the streets. If you didn't understand how the system worked, you were doomed to be exploited by it. But what struck me most was when she said that not everyone was playing to win—some were just playing to keep others from winning. That insight hit me hard. It was as if she had unlocked a piece of the puzzle I had been trying to put together. The political system wasn't just about two parties vying for power. It was about keeping certain groups dependent, making them believe they couldn't win without the help of their supposed allies.

After our conversation, I realized that being Independent wasn't the right choice for me. It was a neutral position, and I didn't want to be neutral. I wanted to take a stand, to choose a side, and for me, that side was the Republican Party. It was the party that aligned with my values—family structure, self-reliance, integrity, and personal responsibility. I didn't want to sit on the sidelines. I wanted to be part of something greater.

Registering as a Republican

When I turned 18 and registered for Selective Service, I also made the decision to officially register as a Republican. It wasn't a decision I made lightly, but it was one that I never regretted. Even though it wasn't the popular choice in my community, I felt a sense of clarity and purpose. I knew that the Republican Party stood for the values that mattered most to me—family, opportunity, and empowerment.

For me, the Democratic Party represented manipulation and control. They had convinced so many people in my community that they were the only option, but I saw through the facade. The Democrats had mastered the art of keeping Black and Brown communities reliant on them without delivering meaningful change. They positioned themselves as saviors while perpetuating systems that kept us dependent, offering handouts but never opportunities for real self-sufficiency. I wasn't going to buy into that narrative. I wasn't going to be manipulated.

From that point forward, I embraced the Republican Party not as a label, but as a vehicle for the values I believed in: self-reliance, opportunity, and family. Registering as a Republican was more than a political choice—it was a declaration of my belief that the future of my community depended on us reclaiming our autonomy, not relying on anyone else to fix our problems.

Challenging the Political Status Quo

Once I officially became a Republican, I felt more empowered to challenge the political status quo in my community. I knew it wouldn't be easy. Most people around me didn't understand why I had made that choice. To them, being a Democrat was as much a part of their identity as the color of their skin. The thought of someone in our community registering as a Republican was almost unthinkable. People would say things like, "Why would you want to be part of the party that doesn't care about us?" The irony is that I saw it the other way around.

I understood that most people weren't thinking critically about their political alignment. They were doing what they had always done, following a tradition passed down from generation to generation without ever questioning whether it still served them. That's what frustrated me the most. The manipulation ran so deep that many in my community didn't even realize they were being used for their votes without ever seeing any real progress in return.

I started having conversations with people around me, asking them tough questions. "Why are you a Democrat? What has the party actually done to improve our lives? Have you ever considered that there might be other options?" I wasn't trying to convert anyone to the Republican Party, but I wanted them to think critically. I wanted them to realize that they didn't have to follow the same political path just because that's what their parents or grandparents had done.

Many of those conversations were difficult. Some people shut me down immediately, dismissing me as a traitor to my race or someone who didn't understand the struggles of our people. But I understood better than they realized. I had lived through those struggles. I had seen firsthand how the promises of politicians didn't translate into meaningful change. I wasn't turning my back on my community—I was trying to wake them up to the reality that there were other paths to empowerment.

The Importance of Family Structure

One of the most significant reasons I aligned with the Republican Party was their emphasis on family structure. To me, family is the foundation of any strong society, and it's something that I believe is under attack in many communities, especially in the Black community. The breakdown of the family unit has led to so many of the issues we see today—poverty, crime, addiction, and a lack of guidance for young people.

The Democratic Party, in my view, had failed to protect and support the family structure. Instead, they had pushed policies that I felt contributed to its breakdown. From welfare programs that discouraged two-parent households to cultural narratives that devalued fatherhood, I saw a pattern of undermining the very institution that holds communities together.

On the other hand, the Republican Party emphasized the importance of strong families, personal responsibility, and self-reliance. These were the values that my father had instilled in me, and I knew that they were the values that would help lift up our community. I believe that when families are strong, communities are strong. When fathers are present, when parents are engaged, when children are raised with discipline and love, the entire community benefits.

This isn't just theoretical for me—I've seen it play out in real life. Growing up, I saw the difference between kids who had strong family support and those who didn't. The kids who had parents who were involved, who held them accountable, and who gave them a sense of structure were far less likely to fall into the traps of the streets. The kids who didn't have that support were often the ones who ended up getting caught up in crime, drugs, or violence.

Family isn't just a political talking point for me. It's the cornerstone of everything I believe in. I knew that if I wanted to see real change in my community, it had to start with strengthening families. That's why I couldn't align myself with a party that seemed to prioritize government dependence over family independence. I wanted to be part of a movement that empowered families to stand on their own, to raise their children with values and discipline, and to create the foundation for success.

Understanding the Stakes

As I got deeper into my political journey, I realized just how high the stakes were. Politics wasn't just about parties and elections—it was about the future of our communities and our country. I began to see that the decisions we make at the ballot box have far-reaching consequences, not just for our own lives but for future generations.

For me, voting Republican wasn't just about the here and now. It was about securing a future where my children and grandchildren would have the opportunity to succeed, where they wouldn't have to rely on the government to take care of them, and where they would have the freedom to pursue their dreams without being held back by a system designed to keep them in place.

One of the most powerful realizations I had was that the Democratic Party didn't really want us to succeed. If we succeeded—if we became truly self-reliant and independent— they would lose their grip on us. Their power was built on keeping communities dependent on government programs, on convincing people that they needed the Democrats to survive. But I knew that wasn't true. We didn't need them. We needed strong families, strong communities, and the freedom to chart our own course.

Facing Resistance

As I became more vocal about my political beliefs, I faced resistance—not just from my community, but from friends and even some family members. They couldn't understand why I had chosen to align with the Republican Party, a party that they saw as hostile to minorities. They believed the narrative that had been pushed for so long—that the Republicans didn't care about Black and Brown people, that they were only for the rich and privileged.

But I saw it differently. To me, the Republican Party wasn't about race—it was about values. It was about opportunity, family, and freedom. I didn't buy into the idea that the Republicans were the enemy of Black people. In fact, I believed they were the ones who offered us the tools we needed to break free from the cycle of dependence that had trapped so many of us for so long.

The resistance I faced only strengthened my resolve. I knew that what I was fighting for was bigger than myself. I was fighting for a future where my community didn't have to rely on anyone else for their success. I was fighting for a future where we could build our own businesses, raise our own families, and live our own lives without interference from politicians who only cared about our votes.

Staying True to My Convictions

Despite the challenges and the push back, I have never regretted my decision to align with the Republican Party. Over the years, I've watched as different presidents and political leaders have come and gone. I've seen policies change, and I've seen the shifting dynamics of the political landscape. But through it all, I've remained committed to the values that first drew me to the Republican Party.

I believe in personal responsibility. I believe in the power of family. I believe in the importance of opportunity and self-reliance. These are the values that have guided me throughout my life, and they are the values that I will continue to fight for.

No matter who is in office, no matter what the political climate may be, I will always stand for what I believe in. I will always challenge the status quo, and I will always encourage others to think critically about their political choices. Because in the end, it's not about following a party—it's about standing up for what you know is right.

A Lifelong Commitment to Political Engagement

Since the day I registered as a Republican, I've never wavered in my commitment to political engagement. Politics is not just something that happens every four years during an election— it's an ongoing process. It's about staying informed, staying involved, and never losing sight of the bigger picture.

For me, politics isn't just about voting—it's about taking action. It's about working in my community to uplift others, to strengthen families, and to create opportunities for those who are willing to work for them. It's about mentoring young people, helping them understand that their future is in their hands, not the hands of politicians or government programs.

As I continue on this journey, I remain dedicated to the principles that have guided me from the beginning: family, opportunity, and personal responsibility. These are the values that will lead us to a better future—not just for me, but for my community, and for future generations.

In the end, my political awakening was about more than just choosing a party—it was about choosing a path. A path of independence, of empowerment, and of self-reliance. And that's a path I will walk for the rest of my life.

Moving Forward

Looking back on my journey into politics, I realize that the lessons I've learned are not just for me—they are for anyone willing to listen, willing to question, and willing to challenge the narratives that have been handed to them. We all have the power to make choices that align with our values, and we all have the responsibility to think critically about the world around us.

I hope that my story inspires others to embark on their own political journeys, to ask the hard questions, and to stand up for what they believe in, even when it's not popular. We live in a world where political identity can feel like a trap—where it seems like you must choose between two options, neither of which fully aligns with your values. But I want people to know that there is always another option: the option to think for yourself, to carve out your own path, and to choose principles over politics.

The Power of Independent Thought

One of the most important lessons I've learned from my political awakening is the power of independent thought. It's easy to get swept up in the current of popular opinion, to go along with what everyone around you believes simply because it's the path of least resistance. But real change, real progress, only happens when people are willing to break away from the herd and challenge the status quo.

For me, that meant questioning the political affiliations that had been passed down through generations in my community. It meant asking why so many people blindly followed the Democratic Party without ever questioning whether it was truly serving their needs. It meant looking at the history of both parties and making an informed decision based on facts, not emotions or traditions.

Independent thought doesn't just apply to politics—it applies to every aspect of life. Whether it's in your career, your personal relationships, or your community, the ability to think critically and make decisions for yourself is invaluable. It's what allows you to take control of your own destiny, rather than letting others dictate the course of your life.

I want to encourage everyone reading this to embrace the power of independent thought. Don't be afraid to question the narratives that have been handed to you. Don't be afraid to stand alone if necessary. It may not always be easy, but it's the only way to truly live a life of integrity and purpose.

Encouraging Dialogue and Understanding

As I've continued on my political journey, I've realized that one of the biggest obstacles to progress is a lack of understanding and dialogue between people with differing political views. Too often, we retreat into our own echo chambers, surrounding ourselves with people who think like us and shutting out anyone who disagrees. This kind of division only deepens the political and social rifts in our society.

One of the things I've always valued about my upbringing was the emphasis on dialogue. My father's discussions with his friends, where they debated politics, culture, and religion, were a formative part of my political education. They taught me that it's possible to disagree with someone without disrespecting them. They showed me that debate and discussion are healthy, and that they are essential to a functioning democracy.

As I've become more politically active, I've tried to foster that same spirit of dialogue. I want people to feel comfortable engaging in conversations about politics, even if they don't agree with me. I believe that when we listen to each other, when we try to understand where the other person is coming from, we can find common ground. We may not always agree, but we can at least come away with a deeper understanding of each other's perspectives.

It's through dialogue that we grow, that we learn, and that we build bridges instead of walls. And in a time when our country feels more divided than ever, I believe that fostering open, honest conversations is one of the most important things we can do.

The Future of Political Engagement

As I look to the future, I see both challenges and opportunities for political engagement. On one hand, we are living in a time of great political polarization, where people are increasingly divided along party lines. On the other hand, we are also seeing a growing movement of people who are tired of the old ways of doing things—people who are hungry for something different, for a new kind of political engagement that is less about parties and more about principles.

I believe that the future of political engagement lies in empowering individuals to take responsibility for their own lives and their own communities. It's about encouraging people to get involved, not just in national politics, but in local politics as well. It's at the local level where we can often have the most direct impact, where we can see the results of our efforts in real-time.

Whether it's running for local office, volunteering in your community, or simply staying informed about the issues that matter to you, political engagement is about more than just voting every four years. It's about being an active participant in shaping the world around you, every day.

For me, that means continuing to speak out about the issues that matter to me, continuing to mentor young people, and continuing to challenge the political narratives that I believe are holding my community back. It means staying true to the values that have guided me throughout my life—family, opportunity, and personal responsibility—and working to ensure that those values are passed down to the next generation.

A Call to Action

As I bring this chapter to a close, I want to leave you with a call to action. No matter where you are on your political journey, whether you're just starting to question the narratives you've been handed or you've been actively engaged in politics for years, I want to encourage you to take the next step.

If you're feeling disillusioned with the current political system, don't give up. If you're feeling like your voice doesn't matter, don't stay silent. We all have the power to make a difference, but that power only comes when we choose to use it.

I challenge you to think critically about the political decisions you make. Don't just vote for a party because that's what you've always done. Do your research. Understand the history. Look at the policies and the values behind the rhetoric. And most importantly, think about what kind of future you want to create—not just for yourself, but for your family, your community, and the generations that will come after you.

If you believe in the importance of family, of opportunity, of personal responsibility, then find a way to support those values in your own life and in the political decisions you make. It's not about following a party—it's about standing for something greater.

Conclusion: The Journey Continues

My political awakening was just the beginning of a lifelong journey. It opened my eyes to the complexities of the political system, but it also gave me a sense of purpose and direction. I realized that I wasn't just a spectator in the world of politics—I was a participant. And with that participation came a responsibility to stay informed, to stay involved, and to fight for the values I believed in.

I've learned that politics isn't about choosing sides—it's

about choosing principles. It's about understanding that the decisions we make today will shape the future for generations to come. And it's about knowing that each of us has the power to make a difference, no matter how small our actions may seem.

So as I continue on this journey, I remain committed to the values that have guided me from the beginning: family, opportunity, and personal responsibility. These are the values that will continue to guide me, and these are the values I hope to pass on to others.

The journey is far from over. There will be challenges ahead, but there will also be opportunities—opportunities to build a better future, to strengthen our communities, and to empower the next generation. And I'm ready to face those challenges head-on, with the same determination and resolve that first led me into the world of politics.

This is my story, but it's also the story of so many others who are waking up to the realities of the political system and choosing to think for themselves. I hope that my journey inspires you to take a closer look at your own beliefs, to question the narratives you've been handed, and to find your own path—one that aligns with your values and your vision for the future. Because in the end, that's what politics is really about: not just choosing a party, but choosing the kind of world you want to create.

Chapter Four: A Journey Through My Lifetime of Presidencies—From Carter to Biden

Surviving five decades of life and witnessing the shifting tides of American politics has given me a unique perspective on the evolution of leadership in this country. The U.S. political landscape, often unpredictable, has profoundly shaped not only the direction of the nation but also the lives of its citizens. My understanding of the intricacies of American politics comes not only from books and news reports but from the lived experience of growing up during times of war, economic prosperity, crises, social movements, and political upheavals.

From Jimmy Carter's presidency to Joe Biden's administration, I have had a front-row seat to watch the transformation of the United States—both its successes and failures. These changes have not only influenced the nation's domestic and international standing but have also impacted everyday people like me, growing up in the urban fabric of Boston, witnessing firsthand the effects of policies implemented by different leaders.

America's history is steeped in contradiction—a nation built on the ideals of freedom, yet historically grounded in the enslavement and oppression of African people, Indigenous populations, and other marginalized groups. Despite the cruelty of these injustices, we are here now, and there's no turning back. The question that remains is: How do we move forward, learning from the lessons of the past while shaping a more equitable and prosperous future? Throughout the presidencies I've witnessed, this tension has defined much of the American experience.

Growing Up Amid Political Shifts: The 1970s and Jimmy Carter (1977–1981)

The 1970s were a time of significant change. The nation was healing from the aftermath of the Vietnam War, the political turmoil of the Watergate scandal, and the social upheaval of the 1960s. Jimmy Carter, elected in 1976, entered the White House during a time of national uncertainty. Carter represented an effort to restore moral leadership to the presidency. A former governor of Georgia, Carter's folksy demeanor and commit-ment to civil rights resonated with many in communities like mine. He spoke about love, justice, and fairness, themes that felt comforting in the aftermath of the chaos of the Nixon years.

Carter's foreign policy, particularly the Camp David Accords, which brokered peace between Israel and Egypt, demonstrated his commitment to diplomacy and peace. This was a significant achievement, earning him respect globally. However, domestically, Carter struggled. The energy crisis, exacerbated by the oil embargo, made life harder for working-class families. Gas prices soared, and inflation skyrocketed, leading to a period known as "stagflation"—a troubling combination of stagnant economic growth and high inflation.

The impact of the economy was palpable in my neighborhood. As a young boy, I remember hearing adults talk about how everything seemed to be getting more expensive. Carter's administration was unable to find a way to stabilize the economy, and his perceived inability to manage the Iran Hostage Crisis, in which 52 Americans were held hostage for 444 days, solidified the public's frustration with his leadership. In 1980, Ronald Reagan won the presidency in a landslide, signaling a clear rejection of Carter's leadership.

Ronald Reagan: An Era of Prosperity and Deep Division (1981–1989)

Ronald Reagan's presidency represented a major shift in American politics. With his charisma and optimism, Reagan promised to restore American pride and leadership. To many, Reagan's vision was one of hope—a stark contrast to the economic malaise of the 1970s. His economic policy, known as "Reaganomics," was based on the principle of supply-side economics, advocating for tax cuts, deregulation, and reduced government spending. The belief was that lowering taxes on corporations and the wealthy would "trickle down" to the working class through job creation and investment.

In some ways, Reaganomics worked. The economy grew, and unemployment rates dropped. For those who were already somewhat stable, Reagan's policies opened up opportunities for financial growth. Business thrived, and many Americans saw improvements in their standard of living. However, the benefits were not evenly distributed. In communities like mine, the wealth gap widened. The rich were getting richer, while the poor were left behind, struggling to make ends meet. The disparity was clear, and it seemed like Reagan's America was only working for the privileged few.

Reagan's presidency also oversaw the start of the Crack Epidemic, which devastated Black and Brown communities. Instead of addressing the root causes of addiction and poverty, Reagan launched the "War on Drugs," which criminalized addiction and disproportionately targeted Black men. I watched as families in my neighborhood were torn apart by mass incarceration. It wasn't just the drug dealers who got caught in the system—it was the users, the addicts, and the people trying to survive in an economy that didn't seem to have room for them.

The War on Drugs led to a significant rise in incarceration rates, and many of the young men I grew up with found themselves locked up for non-violent drug offenses. This wasn't just a war on drugs—it was a war on my community. The long-term effects of Reagan's policies on urban communities are still being felt today.

Despite these issues, Reagan was also credited with ending the Cold War. His diplomatic relationship with Soviet leader Mikhail Gorbachev, including the signing of the Intermediate-Range Nuclear Forces Treaty (INF), helped reduce the nuclear threat and paved the way for the eventual dissolution of the Soviet Union. On the world stage, Reagan was seen as a strong leader, but at home, his policies were leaving behind those who needed the most help.

Video Links:

https://youtube.com/shorts/pFj8JUDb_Yo?si=8Az-YCShcm emBNXC

George H.W. Bush: The War Strategist and Economic Downfall (1989–1993)

When George H.W. Bush took office in 1989, he inherited many of the successes and challenges of the Reagan era. Bush, a former vice president under Reagan, was seen as a seasoned politician, particularly in foreign affairs. His handling of the Gulf War in 1990, when Iraq's Saddam Hussein invaded Kuwait, showcased his strategic leadership. Bush built a broad coalition of international allies, executed a swift military campaign, and successfully liberated Kuwait. His approval ratings soared, and many Americans saw him as a strong, capable leader.

But Bush's presidency, like Carter's, was marred by economic troubles. The early 1990s recession hit hard, and Bush's decision to raise taxes, despite his famous campaign promise of "no new taxes," alienated many within his party. The economic downturn led to widespread dissatisfaction, and by 1992, many Americans were ready for a change.

Bill Clinton: Economic Boom and Political Scandal (1993–2001)

Bill Clinton's presidency ushered in a period of economic growth and optimism. The 1990s are often remembered as a time of technological innovation, with the dot-com boom transforming the economy. Clinton's policies, including the expansion of the Earned Income Tax Credit and welfare reform, helped lift many Americans out of poverty. Unemployment rates dropped, and the stock market soared. It seemed, for a time, that the American Dream was within reach for more people than ever before.

I remember feeling a sense of economic security during Clinton's presidency. Jobs were plentiful, and for the first time in a long time, people in my community felt like they had a shot at upward mobility. But while the economy thrived, other issues lurked beneath the surface.

The 1994 Crime Bill, signed into law by Clinton, had a devastating impact on Black and Brown communities. Building on Reagan's War on Drugs, the bill expanded mass incarceration, particularly for non-violent drug offenses. My community, already struggling from the effects of the Crack Epidemic, was further devastated by this legislation. Clinton's tough-on-crime policies may have been politically popular, but they disproportionately targeted people of color, leading to the incarceration of millions of Black men.

Then there was the Monica Lewinsky scandal. Clinton's affair with a White House intern and the subsequent impeachment trial dominated the headlines for months. The scandal turned the presidency into a spectacle, distracting from the substantive issues facing the country. Despite the controversy, Clinton left office with high approval ratings, buoyed by the economic boom of the 1990s.

George W. Bush: War and Economic Collapse (2001–2009)

The 2000 election between George W. Bush and Al Gore was one of the most contested in U.S. history, culminating in a Supreme Court decision that effectively handed Bush the presidency. The country was deeply divided, and Bush's presidency would only become more controversial as time went on.

The defining moment of Bush's presidency was, without a doubt, the September 11th terrorist attacks in 2001. I remember that day vividly—the shock, the fear, and the sense that the world had changed forever. In the aftermath of the attacks, Bush led the nation with a steady hand, and for a brief moment, the country came together. His decision to invade Afghanistan, where the Taliban was harboring AL-Qaeda leader Osama bin Laden, was widely supported.

However, Bush's decision to invade Iraq in 2003, based on the false claim that Saddam Hussein possessed weapons of mass destruction, became one of the most controversial foreign policy decisions in modern history. The Iraq War destabilized the Middle East and cost thousands of American lives. It also drained the U.S. economy, contributing to the national debt and undermining Bush's domestic agenda.

The final years of Bush's presidency were defined by the 2008 financial crisis. The housing bubble burst, leading to a global economic meltdown. Millions of Americans lost their homes, their jobs, and their savings. By the time Bush left office, his approval ratings had plummeted, and the country was in desperate need of change.

Barack Obama: A Hopeful Beginning and a Complicated Legacy (2009–2017)

When Barack Obama was elected president in 2008, it felt like a new era had begun. Obama's election was historic— he was the first Black president, and for many, his victory symbolized a turning point in America's racial history. The excitement surrounding Obama's candidacy was palpable. His message of hope and change resonated deeply, especially for communities that had long been marginalized and excluded from the political process. For the first time in my life, I felt like there was a chance for real progress—a chance for America to finally live up to its ideals of equality and justice for all.

I was one of the millions who voted for Barack Obama in 2008, inspired by his promise to bring about meaningful change. His eloquence, intelligence, and optimism made him a beacon of hope during a time of economic crisis and social unrest. The country was reeling from the Great Recession, and people were looking for a leader who could steer the ship back on course.

Obama's first major legislative victory was the passage of the American Recovery and Reinvestment Act, a massive stimulus package designed to jump-start the economy in the aftermath of the financial crisis. The stimulus provided funding for infrastructure projects, education, healthcare, and renewable energy. While it did help stabilize the economy and prevent a deeper depression, it wasn't enough to alleviate the pain many Americans were feeling, particularly those in working-class and minority communities.

The Affordable Care Act: A Mixed Bag

One of the defining moments of Obama's presidency was the passage of the Affordable Care Act (ACA), also known as Obamacare. The ACA aimed to expand healthcare coverage to millions of uninsured Americans and make healthcare more affordable. It was a landmark piece of legislation that represented a significant step toward universal healthcare, something progressive activists had been fighting for for decades.

However, the roll out of Obamacare was fraught with challenges. The website launch was a disaster, with technical glitches preventing people from signing up for coverage. Moreover, the mandate requiring individuals to purchase health insurance or face a penalty was deeply unpopular, especially among working-class Americans who were already struggling to make ends meet. Many felt that the law forced them to buy insurance they couldn't afford, without providing enough relief for the rising costs of premiums and deductibles.

While the ACA did expand coverage to millions of people and eliminated some of the worst practices of the insurance industry—such as denying coverage based on preexisting conditions—it also left many feeling frustrated and disillusioned. For some, Obama's healthcare law was a lifeline; for others, it was an overreach of government that imposed additional financial burdens on already struggling families.

The Promise of Criminal Justice Reform

One of the areas where I felt Obama had real potential to make a difference was in criminal justice reform. As a Black man, I had witnessed firsthand the devastating effects of mass incarceration on my community. The legacy of the War on Drugs and the tough-on-crime policies of previous administrations had disproportionately impacted Black and Brown people, leading to the over-policing and over-incarceration of non-violent offenders.

During his presidency, Obama took steps to address these issues. He commuted the sentences of hundreds of non-violent drug offenders, and his administration supported efforts to reduce mandatory minimum sentences for certain drug crimes. In 2015, Obama became the first sitting president to visit a federal prison, signaling his commitment to reforming a broken system.

However, despite these efforts, Obama's legacy on criminal justice reform remains complicated. While he made strides in addressing some of the worst excesses of the criminal justice system, many of the structural issues—such as racial profiling, police violence, and the prison-industrial complex—persisted. The rise of the Black Lives Matter movement during Obama's presidency highlighted the continued struggle for racial justice and police accountability, underscoring the fact that progress was slow and often incomplete.

Foreign Policy and the Legacy of War

On the international stage, Obama's foreign policy was a mixed bag. He inherited two wars—one in Iraq and one in Afghanistan—and campaigned on a promise to end them. In 2011, Obama oversaw the withdrawal of U.S. troops from Iraq, fulfilling a key campaign promise. However, the rise of the Islamic State (ISIS) in the aftermath of the U.S. withdrawal led to renewed conflict in the region, and by 2014, Obama had authorized airstrikes and the deployment of troops to combat ISIS.

In Afghanistan, Obama increased the U.S. military presence in what became known as the "Afghan surge." While this strategy aimed to stabilize the country and weaken the Taliban, the war dragged on throughout Obama's presidency, with no clear resolution in sight.

One of Obama's most significant foreign policy achievements was the operation that resulted in the killing of Osama bin Laden, the mastermind behind the September 11th attacks. The successful raid on bin Laden's compound in Pakistan was a major victory for the Obama administration and provided a sense of closure for many Americans still reeling from the trauma of 9/11.

However, Obama's use of drone warfare and targeted killings in countries like Yemen, Pakistan, and Somalia raised ethical concerns. While the administration argued that drones were a more precise and less costly alternative to conventional warfare, the program resulted in significant civilian casualties and was criticized for its lack of transparency and accountability.

The Economic Recovery and the Frustration of Many

While Obama was able to prevent the U.S. economy from spiraling into a full-blown depression, the recovery was uneven. Wall Street rebounded quickly, and the stock market reached new heights, but the benefits of the recovery didn't trickle down to working-class Americans in the way many had hoped. Wages remained stagnant, and economic inequality continued to grow.

I remember feeling a sense of frustration during this time. For all of Obama's talk about helping the middle class and providing economic opportunity for all, it often felt like the wealthy were the ones benefiting most from his policies. The bailout of Wall Street banks and the auto industry may have been necessary to stabilize the economy, but it left many ordinary Americans feeling abandoned. Instead of getting direct relief, the working class was left to pick up the pieces while corporate America thrived.

The Rise of Donald Trump: A Nation Divided (2017–2021)

By the time the 2016 election rolled around, the country was more divided than I had ever seen it. The election of Donald Trump represented a seismic shift in American politics. Trump's populist message resonated with many Americans who felt left behind by the political establishment. He promised to "drain the swamp," bring back jobs, and put America first. His rhetoric was brash, and his approach unconventional, but for many voters, that was precisely what made him appealing.

Trump's victory was a shock to the system, and for many in the political elite, it was an unfathomable outcome. But to me, it wasn't all that surprising. Trump tapped into a deep well of discontent that had been brewing for years—discontent with economic stagnation, with cultural elites, and with a political class that seemed out of touch with the concerns of ordinary Americans.

I watched as Trump's presidency unfolded, marked by both successes and controversies. On the economic front, Trump delivered on many of his promises. Unemployment rates dropped to record lows, and for the first time in years, wage growth began to pick up. His tax cuts, while criticized by some for disproportionately benefiting the wealthy, provided relief for many small business owners and working-class Americans.

Trump's focus on energy independence and deregulation helped lower energy costs and boosted domestic production. Under his administration, the U.S. became a net exporter of oil for the first time in decades, reducing the nation's reliance on foreign energy sources.

However, Trump's presidency was also defined by chaos and division. His polarizing style and combative approach to politics alienated many, and his handling of the COVID-19 pandemic was widely criticized. While Operation Warp Speed, the initiative to fast-track the development of COVID-19 vaccines, was a major success, but the credit he deserved fell flat because of the hate he endured.

The COVID-19 Pandemic and Economic Turmoil

The COVID-19 pandemic was a crisis unlike any other in modern history, and it tested the limits of the U.S. government's ability to respond to a public health emergency. The pandemic brought the global economy to a standstill, and millions of Americans found themselves out of work as businesses shut down and industries collapsed.

Trump's administration responded with the Paycheck Protection Program (PPP), which provided loans to small businesses to help them keep their employees on the payroll. The program helped many businesses survive, but the economic impact of the pandemic was devastating, particularly for low-wage workers and minority communities.

The pandemic also highlighted the deep racial and economic disparities in the U.S. healthcare system. Black and Brown communities were disproportionately affected by the virus, both in terms of infection rates and fatalities. The economic fallout further exacerbated these inequalities, as many people of color worked in essential jobs that put them at greater risk of exposure.

Joe Biden: A Struggling Presidency (2021–Present)

Joe Biden's presidency began amid unprecedented challenges. The nation was still reeling from the pandemic, and the political climate was as polarized as ever. Biden campaigned on a promise to "restore the soul of the nation" and bring the country together after the divisive Trump years. But so far, his presidency has been marked by economic struggles, rising inflation, and a series of political crises that have left many Americans feeling disillusioned.

From the beginning, Biden faced the enormous task of stabilizing an economy battered by the pandemic. His administration passed a massive stimulus package, the American Rescue Plan, designed to provide relief to struggling Americans and support the ongoing recovery. However, rather than ushering in a return to normalcy, Biden's policies seemed to compound existing problems, particularly with inflation, which reached levels not seen in decades.

Gas prices soared under Biden's leadership, in part due to his administration's restrictions on domestic energy production and the cancellation of projects like the Keystone XL pipeline. For families already struggling to make ends meet, these rising costs only added to their financial burdens. The economy, which had shown signs of recovery under Trump, began to falter under Biden's administration, leading to widespread dissatisfaction. Inflation, particularly the rise in prices for essential goods like groceries and gasoline, hit working- and middle-class families the hardest. The promise of economic recovery seemed distant for many, as wages remained stagnant while the cost of living continued to climb. This economic decline under Biden's watch fueled growing frustrations, especially among those who had placed their hopes in him to restore stability and prosperity.

The Struggle for Unity Amid Polarization

One of Biden's central campaign promises was to restore unity to a deeply divided nation. He spoke frequently of healing the divisions that had been exacerbated during the Trump years and fostering a sense of national unity. However, the reality of his presidency has been anything but unifying. Partisan divisions have only deepened, with both Democrats and Republicans retreating further into their respective camps. The culture wars that had raged during Trump's tenure intensified under Biden, particularly around issues like critical race theory, LGBTQ+ rights, and immigration.

Biden's administration, while attempting to push forward an agenda that addressed these cultural and social issues, found itself caught in the crossfire. Rather than bringing the country together, these issues became flash points for even greater political polarization. Debates over race, gender, and identity took center stage, and the national discourse became increasingly hostile. Biden's attempts at unity were drowned out by the noise of social media outrage and partisan bickering.

The Border Crisis and National Security Concerns

Biden's presidency has also been marked by a worsening crisis at the U.S.-Mexico border. His decision to roll back many of Trump's immigration policies, including halting construction of the border wall and softening enforcement measures, led to a significant surge in illegal immigration. Border facilities were overwhelmed as record numbers of migrants attempted to cross into the United States. Images of overcrowded detention centers and reports of inhumane conditions dominated the news, fueling criticism of the administration's handling of the crisis.

For many Americans, the border crisis became a symbol of the Biden administration's inability to manage national security effectively. While Biden campaigned on promises of compassion and a more humane immigration system, the reality on the ground told a different story. The administration's failure to address the situation quickly and efficiently led to a sense of insecurity, with concerns about the potential for increased crime, drug trafficking, and strained social services.

Compounding this issue was the Biden administration's chaotic withdrawal of U.S. troops from Afghanistan in August 2021. The withdrawal, which was intended to end America's longest war, quickly devolved into a disaster. The swift takeover of Afghanistan by the Taliban, the images of desperate Afghans clinging to U.S. military planes, and the tragic bombing at the Kabul airport that killed 13 U.S. service members, shocked the world and tarnished Biden's reputation on foreign policy. What was meant to be a moment of closure for the U.S. military turned into a humanitarian crisis and a blow to America's global standing.

Racial Justice and Social Unrest

The racial justice movements that gained prominence during Trump's presidency continued to play a significant role in the national conversation under Biden. The protests and unrest that erupted after the killing of George Floyd in 2020, which were driven by demands for police reform and an end to systemic racism, were still fresh in the minds of many Americans as Biden took office. He made commitments to address racial inequality and advance civil rights, but the results have been mixed.

Biden signed executive orders aimed at addressing racial equity, including one that sought to reform federal law enforcement practices. However, his efforts to pass more sweeping police reform legislation were stymied by a deeply divided Congress. The George Floyd Justice in Policing Act, which aimed to hold law enforcement accountable for misconduct, failed to garner enough bipartisan support, leaving many activists disappointed.

The racial discourse in America, particularly surrounding issues like critical race theory and school curriculum's, became another point of contention. Conservative lawmakers and parents clashed with progressive activists over how race should be taught in schools, leading to heated debates and legislative battles across the country. For many, Biden's administration appeared to struggle in navigating these complex and deeply emotional issues, further highlighting the challenges of governing in a nation so divided.

Economic Policy and the Build Back Better Plan

One of the cornerstone initiatives of Biden's presidency was his "Build Back Better" plan, a sweeping legislative agenda aimed at addressing everything from climate change to healthcare to infrastructure. The plan was ambitious, with trillions of dollars in proposed spending intended to modernize the nation's infrastructure, expand social safety nets, and promote green energy.

However, Biden's ambitious agenda quickly encountered roadblocks. The plan faced resistance not only from Republicans but also from moderate Democrats who were concerned about the price tag and the potential for increased government debt. Despite controlling both the House and Senate, the Biden administration struggled to pass key components of the Build Back Better plan, leading to a series of compromises that watered down the original vision.

While some elements of the plan were eventually passed, including the Infrastructure Investment and Jobs Act, which provided funding for roads, bridges, and broadband, the larger social spending package stalled in Congress. For many progressives, this was a bitter disappointment, as they had hoped Biden's presidency would usher in transformative change on issues like healthcare, climate policy, and child care. For moderates and conservatives, however, the failure to pass the more expansive elements of the plan was seen as a victory against government overreach.

Biden's Foreign Policy Challenges

In addition to the botched withdrawal from Afghanistan, Biden's foreign policy record has been marked by a number of other challenges. His administration has struggled to navigate an increasingly tense relationship with China, particularly over trade issues, human rights abuses, and the growing influence of China in global affairs. Biden has sought to balance a tough stance on China with efforts to maintain diplomatic relations, but the situation remains fraught with tension.

Russia has also been a thorn in Biden's side, particularly with the ongoing conflict in Ukraine. In early 2022, Russian President Vladimir Putin launched a full-scale invasion of Ukraine, prompting international outrage and leading to one of the largest military conflicts in Europe since World War II. Biden responded with a series of economic sanctions against Russia and increased military aid to Ukraine, but the conflict has continued to escalate, with no clear end in sight.

The situation in Ukraine, along with the broader geopolitical challenges posed by China and Russia, has tested Biden's ability to maintain America's position on the global stage. His administration's foreign policy has been criticized as reactive rather than proactive, leaving many to question whether the U.S. is still the global leader it once was.

Biden's Struggles with Public Perception and Approval

As Biden's presidency has progressed, his approval ratings have plummeted. Rising inflation, the ongoing immigration crisis, the Afghanistan debacle, and a series of other challenges have left many Americans questioning his leadership. For those who voted for Biden in the hope of returning to normalcy after the chaos of the Trump years, his presidency has been a disappointment.

Biden's age has also become a point of concern for many voters. At 78, Biden was the oldest person ever elected to the presidency, and questions about his cognitive abilities and physical health have been raised repeatedly by his critics. Despite these concerns, Biden has made it clear that he intends to run for re-election in 2024, though it remains to be seen whether he will garner enough support to secure a second term.

Reflecting on Leadership and Lessons Learned

As I look back on the presidencies I've lived through, from Jimmy Carter to Joe Biden, I'm struck by the ways in which leadership has evolved—and sometimes regressed—over the years. Each president has faced their own unique challenges, and each has left their own mark on the country. Some have inspired hope and progress, while others have deepened divisions and created new problems.

Carter, for all his moral leadership, was unable to overcome the economic and geopolitical challenges of his time. Reagan restored national pride but at the cost of deepening inequality and launching a war on drugs that devastated communities like mine. George H.W. Bush was a skilled diplomat, but his failure to address the domestic economy led to his downfall. Clinton brought economic prosperity, but his policies on crime and welfare reform hurt many marginalized communities. George W. Bush's presidency was defined by war and economic collapse, while Obama's promise of hope and change was often overshadowed by the realities of governing.

Donald Trump brought economic growth and energy independence but was undone by his divisive rhetoric and chaotic leadership style. And now, under Joe Biden, we face a presidency struggling to find its footing amid economic turmoil, social unrest, and global crises.

Moving Forward: The Role of Citizens in Shaping the Future

Through it all, one thing has become abundantly clear: no president can single-handedly solve all of America's problems. Leadership is important, but it is only one piece of the puzzle. The future of this country depends not just on who occupies the Oval Office but on the active engagement of its citizens.

As I've grown older, I've come to understand that real change starts from the ground up. It's the people—ordinary citizens—who have the power to demand accountability, push for policies that benefit everyone, and hold their leaders to a higher standard. We cannot sit idly by and expect the government to fix all of our problems. We must be engaged, informed, and willing to fight for the future we want to create.

In reflecting on the presidencies I've lived through, I see both cautionary tales and glimmers of hope. The path forward won't be easy, but if there's one thing I've learned, it's that the power to shape the future is in our hands. It's up to us to hold our leaders accountable, to demand better, and to work together to build a more just and prosperous America for all.

And so, as the nation continues to grapple with its current challenges, I remain hopeful, but also vigilant. The presidencies I've witnessed—from Carter to Biden—have shown me that leadership, while crucial, is not the ultimate determinant of a nation's success. It's the collective will and action of the people that truly defines the direction a country takes. Every administration, regardless of its political leanings, has had its share of triumphs and failures. Yet, it's the people—those who go to work every day, raise families, volunteer in their communities, and fight for justice—who are the real backbone of this nation.

The Power of Civic Engagement

Looking back at my journey through these presidencies, one of the most important lessons I've learned is the necessity of civic engagement. It's easy to become disillusioned with politics, especially when leaders fail to live up to their promises. But disengagement only serves to strengthen the status quo. The people who are most affected by policies—whether they relate to healthcare, education, criminal justice, or the economy— are often those with the least political power. That needs to change.

When I think about the major social and political shifts in American history, I'm reminded that they didn't come from the top down. The civil rights movement, women's suffrage, labor reforms—these victories were fought and won by ordinary people who demanded change. It wasn't presidents or Congress members who were marching in the streets, enduring violence, or organizing strikes. It was citizens.

As I reflect on the presidencies I've lived through, I've realized that while each president plays a critical role in shaping the nation's direction, real change doesn't happen unless the people demand it. Reagan's tough-on-crime policies, which led to the mass incarceration of Black men, wouldn't have been addressed at all had it not been for activists and citizens pushing for criminal justice reform decades later. Similarly, the racial justice protests during Obama's and Trump's presidencies showed that the people's voice could no longer be ignored.

During Trump's administration, we saw the power of grass-roots organizing with movements like the Women's March and Black Lives Matter. Whether you agreed with these movements or not, they demonstrated that people were no longer content to sit on the sidelines. They were stepping up and demanding that their voices be heard.

Now, under Biden's presidency, that same energy is needed. The economic and social challenges we face are immense, but they are not insurmountable if citizens remain engaged and active. Voting is only the first step in a long process of holding leaders accountable. Civic engagement means staying informed, participating in local government, advocating for policies that benefit the common good, and building coalitions to push for change.

Lessons from the Past, Visions for the Future

The history of presidencies I've lived through offers many lessons—some about the pitfalls of leadership, others about the promise of what's possible when the right choices are made. But if there's one thing I've come to understand, it's that leadership is a partnership between the people and their elected officials. Presidents may set the tone for the nation, but it's the people who shape its soul.

As we move forward, I believe we must take the lessons of the past and use them to build a better future. We must advocate for policies that not only promote economic prosperity but also address systemic inequalities. We need to demand a criminal justice system that truly serves justice, not just punishment. We need leaders who will confront the climate crisis head-on, ensuring that future generations have a planet to call home. We need a healthcare system that prioritizes people over profits, ensuring that no one has to choose between getting medical care and paying rent.

But most importantly, we need to rebuild a sense of unity and common purpose in this country. The polarization that has defined the past several presidencies has made it harder for us to see each other as fellow citizens. Instead, we've been conditioned to view those with opposing political views as enemies. That kind of division weakens the very fabric of democracy.

True leadership, whether it comes from the White House or the streets, involves listening, compromise, and a commitment to the greater good. It means understanding that we're all in this together, whether we like it or not. If there's one thing I've learned from the presidencies of my lifetime, it's that no one leader can fix everything. Real, lasting change requires all of us to roll up our sleeves and get involved.

A Call to Action

The next generation will inherit the consequences of the decisions we make today. As I reflect on my experiences and the presidencies that have shaped my view of the world, I'm reminded that the future is not predetermined. It's shaped by the actions we take in the present. The political landscape may seem daunting, and at times, it's easy to feel powerless. But history has shown us that when people come together, even the most entrenched systems can be transformed.

As citizens, we must take ownership of our role in shaping the future. Whether it's through voting, organizing, advocating for policies, or simply having tough conversations with our neighbors, we have the power to influence the direction of this country. We've seen the highs and lows of leadership through the presidents I've lived under, but if there's one constant, it's that the people always have a voice. It's up to us to decide how we use it.

The journey through the presidencies of Carter, Reagan, Bush, Clinton, Obama, Trump, and Biden has been marked by moments of hope, despair, progress, and setbacks. But through it all, I've learned that the most important leader in any democracy is not the president—it's the people.

As we look to the future, let's remember the lessons of the past. Let's hold our leaders accountable, but let's also hold ourselves accountable. The power to change this nation doesn't rest solely in the hands of those in office. It rests with each and every one of us. If we want a better future, we must be willing to work for it—together.

Conclusion: A Future Built on Hope and Responsibility

The presidencies that have spanned my lifetime represent a microcosm of America's ongoing struggle to balance progress with its past. Each administration has left its imprint on the nation's identity, shaping policies that affected millions of lives. From Carter's idealism to Reagan's economic revolution, from Clinton's prosperity marred by scandal to Obama's promise of hope tempered by compromise, and from Trump's polarizing populism to Biden's efforts to steer the nation through crisis— the arc of leadership in America is complicated and often imperfect.

As I reflect on these leaders, I realize that the most important lesson I've learned is that hope for the future lies not in the hands of any one president but in the collective responsibility of the people. The America I want to see is one where citizens are engaged, where families are strong, where communities are empowered, and where leaders are held accountable for their actions.

The challenges we face are daunting, but I believe in the re-silience of the American people. We've weathered crises before, and we will do so again. But the future will be determined by the choices we make today—choices that require us to rise above partisanship, to embrace our shared humanity, and to work toward a common goal of justice and opportunity for all.

In the end, the journey through my lifetime of presidencies has been one of learning, reflection, and growth. It has shown me that while presidents come and go, the strength of this nation lies in its people. It's up to us to ensure that the next chapter of American history is one defined by unity, progress, and hope. Let's get to work.

Chapter Five: A Republican Journey – Values, Reflections, the Road Less Traveled, and The Weight of History

Growing up, I was surrounded by the influence of the Democratic Party. It was deeply ingrained in the culture of my community, especially among Black and Brown families. For many of us, it seemed like an unspoken rule: to be Black meant to be a Democrat. The party was presented as the voice of the marginalized—the defender of civil rights and the advocate for the working class. But even as a young person, I could sense that something wasn't quite right. There was a disconnect between the promises that Democratic politicians made and the reality on the ground.

The more I listened and observed, the more I realized that the promises made by Democrats often didn't match the results. Sure, they talked a good game—about justice, equality, and opportunity—but in the end, their policies didn't seem to lift us up. Instead, they often left us in the same place or, in some cases, made things worse. It didn't take long for me to start asking questions. Why was my community still struggling after decades of Democratic leadership? Why were so many of us stuck in cycles of poverty, crime, and dependence, despite all the promises of progress?

I started to do my own research, and what I found only confirmed my suspicions. The Democratic Party, which now positioned itself as the champion of minority rights, had a dark history that couldn't be ignored. The Southern Democrats— who once made up the backbone of the party—were the very people who had historically enslaved Black Americans. They were the architects of Jim Crow, the enforcers of segregation, and the perpetrators of lynchings and violence against Black communities. The more I learned, the clearer it became that the same party that now claimed to be our ally had, for much of history, been our oppressor.

A Legacy of Manipulation

When slavery was finally abolished, the oppression of Black people didn't end—it just took on a new form. The physical chains may have been removed, but the chains of Jim Crow and segregation quickly replaced them. These laws were designed to keep Black people in a state of second-class citizenship, preventing us from enjoying the full rights and opportunities that should have been ours as American citizens. The Southern Democrats who controlled state governments used every tool at their disposal—violence, intimidation, and legislation—to maintain their power and keep Black people subjugated.

But the manipulation didn't stop there. In the North, many Black families became Democratic out of necessity. Jobs were scarce, and aligning with Democratic politicians was often the only way to secure employment or access to welfare programs. It wasn't necessarily a choice—it was survival. The Democrats offered jobs, welfare, and social programs, but there was always a hidden cost: dependency. Over time, entire communities became reliant on government assistance, and the Democrats used this dependency to keep their hold on power. The more dependent people became on these programs, the less likely they were to question the system that kept them down.

This realization hit me hard. It made me question everything I had been taught about the Democratic Party. I began to see that their policies weren't designed to uplift us; they were designed to control us. Welfare programs that were supposed to provide temporary relief became a permanent fixture in people's lives, trapping generations in poverty. Government housing projects, meant to provide safe and affordable housing, became breeding grounds for crime and despair. The Democrats, it seemed, weren't offering a hand up—they were offering a cage, disguised as compassion.

A Defining Moment in Dudley Station

By the time I was a teenager, I had already begun to question the political leanings of my community. I knew I didn't want to simply accept the Democratic label that everyone around me seemed to embrace. But at the same time, I hadn't yet found an alternative that spoke to me. The pressure to conform to Democratic ideals was constant, but something in my gut told me that this wasn't the right path for me.

Just before my 18th birthday, I found myself at a crossroads. I was leaning toward becoming Independent. I valued freedom—freedom of thought, freedom of action, and freedom from the constraints of political labels. I didn't want to align myself with any party that tried to pigeonhole me into a particular ideology. Independence felt like the only option that allowed me to think for myself.

Then, one day, I had a conversation that would change the course of my political journey. I was at Dudley Station, waiting for the bus, when I struck up a conversation with a woman who was sitting nearby. She wasn't a politician. She didn't come armed with talking points or campaign slogans. She spoke to me about values—personal responsibility, the importance of family, and the power of self-determination. She talked about how real power came not from government handouts, but from the ability to stand on your own two feet and build something for yourself and your family.

Her words resonated with me on a deep level. It wasn't just what she said, but the way she said it. There was no pretense, no manipulation—just a simple truth that I couldn't ignore. Independence, as appealing as it was, wasn't enough. I needed to stand for something more, and the values she spoke of were the same values I had been raised with. That day at Dudley Station, I made up my mind. I wasn't going to float through life politically unanchored. I was going to become a Republican.

Choosing the Republican Party

When I turned 18 and registered for Selective Service, I had already made my decision—I was a Republican. It wasn't a decision I made lightly. I had thought long and hard about where I stood politically, and in the end, the principles of the Republican Party aligned most closely with my values. I believed in the importance of family, in personal responsibility, and in the idea that government should create opportunities, not dependency.

The Republican Party wasn't perfect, and I knew that. But I didn't need it to be perfect—I needed it to be principled. The Democratic Party's obsession with government intervention and expanding the welfare state left me cold. It seemed to me that they wanted to keep people in a cycle of dependence, offering just enough to keep them loyal, but never enough to truly lift them out of poverty. The Republican Party, on the other hand, emphasized self-reliance. It wasn't about giving handouts; it was about creating an environment where people could succeed through hard work and determination.

Family values were another significant factor in my decision. My father, a man of deep wisdom and integrity, always stressed the importance of family. He was a peaceful and compassionate man who believed that the strength of a society depended on the strength of its families. He taught me that a strong family could withstand any storm, and that personal responsibility was the key to success. The values my father instilled in me were the same values I saw reflected in the Republican Party's platform.

The Role of Faith in Politics

My decision to become a Republican was also deeply influenced by my faith. My father was a peaceful Muslim, and his faith played a central role in shaping his worldview. He believed in personal accountability, in the importance of doing good works, and in the value of self-discipline. These principles of faith aligned closely with the values of the Republican Party, particularly when it came to issues like personal responsibility and the role of government in people's lives.

For me, faith and politics are intertwined. I believe that a society is only as strong as the moral character of its people, and that government should reflect those values. The Republican Party's emphasis on family, faith, and individual liberty resonated with me in a way that the Democratic Party's policies never did. While the Democrats talked about justice and equality, their solutions often involved expanding government power at the expense of personal freedom and responsibility.

Why I Still Stand with the Republican Party

To this day, people often ask me how I can remain a Republican when so many people of color align themselves with the Democratic Party. It's a question I've heard countless times, and I understand why people ask it. After all, the media and popular culture often paint the Democratic Party as the party of diversity and inclusion, while the Republican Party is framed as the party of the wealthy, the privileged, and the white. But that framing is a distortion—a caricature that doesn't reflect the reality of what the Republican Party stands for.

At its core, the Republican Party is about empowering individuals to take control of their own lives. It's about creating an environment where people can thrive without the heavy hand of government interference. That's why I support the party. I don't need the government to give me anything. What I need is for the government to step aside and let me work, let me build, and let me create my own future.

The Democratic Party, for all its talk about diversity and inclusion, often seems more interested in keeping people dependent on government programs than in empowering them to succeed on their own. Welfare, food stamps, government housing—these programs may provide temporary relief, but they don't offer a path to real independence. The Republican Party, by contrast, believes in creating opportunities for people to succeed through their own efforts. That's a message I can stand behind.

The Road Less Traveled

Choosing to be a Republican as a Black man in America hasn't always been easy. There's an expectation in our communities that we align ourselves with the Democratic Party, no questions asked. But I've never been one to follow the crowd. I make my decisions based on what I believe is right, not what's popular. And for me, the Republican Party represents the values that matter most: family, faith, and freedom.

It's not an easy road. I've faced criticism, skepticism, and outright hostility for my political beliefs. But I have never wavered in my convictions. I stand by my decision to be a Republican because it reflects who I am, the values I hold dear, and the lessons I've learned from my life and my family. The path I've chosen is not the easiest, but it's the one that feels most honest and true to me. I've never been one to take the easy road, and I'm not about to start now.

Being a Republican as a Black man means navigating spaces where I sometimes feel outnumbered or misunderstood. But I'm not deterred by that. In fact, it strengthens my resolve. When I engage in political discussions, whether it's with family members, friends, or colleagues, I often encounter people who believe that because of my race, I should automatically align with the Democratic Party. It's as if they see my political identity as predetermined by the color of my skin rather than the content of my character or the values I hold dear. But I refuse to be boxed in like that.

The Weight of History

There's a weight that comes with political choices, especially when you belong to a group that has historically been marginalized and oppressed. The weight of history is always present, and it influences the decisions we make, whether consciously or unconsciously. As a Black man, I'm acutely aware of the struggles that my ancestors endured—the horrors of slavery, the degradation of Jim Crow, the fight for civil rights. That history is part of me, and I carry it with me every day.

But I also understand that history doesn't define me. I'm not bound by the choices that previous generations made, and I'm not obligated to follow the same political path just because that's what's expected. The weight of history is real, but so is the power of choice. And I choose to align myself with the party that I believe offers the best path forward for me, my family, and my community.

When I look back at the history of the Republican Party, I see a legacy that is often misunderstood or ignored. It was the Republican Party that fought to end slavery and that championed civil rights during the Reconstruction era. Abraham Lincoln, the first Republican president, signed the Emancipation Proclamation, and it was the Republican Party that pushed for the 13th, 14th, and 15th Amendments to the Constitution, which abolished slavery, guaranteed equal protection under the law, and secured voting rights for Black Americans.

Of course, the Republican Party of today is different from the Republican Party of Lincoln's time, just as the Democratic Party has undergone significant changes since the days of the Southern segregationists. But the values that drew me to the Republican Party—freedom, personal responsibility, and opportunity—are the same values that inspired the party's founding. And those values are as relevant today as they were in the 19th century.

The Challenge of Defying Expectations

One of the biggest challenges of being a Black Republican is the constant pressure to justify my political choices. People often assume that because of my race, I should automatically vote Democrat. When I explain my reasons for supporting the Republican Party, I'm often met with confusion or skepticism. "How can you support a party that doesn't care about Black people?" they ask. Or, "How can you be part of a party that's so often associated with racism and discrimination?"

These are fair questions, and I don't shy away from answering them. I understand why people might feel that way, especially given the way the media often portrays the Republican Party. But I also know that the reality is more nuanced than the headlines suggest. The Republican Party isn't monolithic, just as the Democratic Party isn't. There are Republicans who are deeply committed to racial justice, to reforming the criminal justice system, and to creating economic opportunities for communities of color. And there are Democrats whose policies, while well-intention, have done more harm than good.

The truth is, neither party has a monopoly on morality or justice. Both parties have their flaws, and both have made mistakes. But for me, the Republican Party represents the best chance for creating the kind of future I want to see—a future where individuals are empowered to succeed on their own terms, where families are strong, and where government plays a supporting role rather than a controlling one.

A Commitment to Personal Responsibility

At the heart of my decision to be a Republican is my commitment to personal responsibility. This is a value that was instilled in me by my father, who taught me that no one is going to hand you success—you have to work for it. He believed in the importance of hard work, discipline, and perseverance, and he lived those values every day. He didn't rely on the government to provide for him or his family; he took responsibility for his own success, and he taught me to do the same.

This is one of the reasons I resonate with the Republican Party's emphasis on self-reliance. I don't believe that government handouts are the solution to poverty or inequality. In fact, I think they often do more harm than good by creating dependency and stifling initiative. What people need are opportunities—opportunities to work, to build, to create, and to succeed on their own terms. And that's what the Republican Party stands for: creating an environment where individuals can thrive without being held back by government overreach.

Family Values: The Foundation of Success

Another reason I align with the Republican Party is its commitment to family values. I've always believed that the strength of a society is rooted in the strength of its families. Without strong families, communities fall apart. That's something I've seen firsthand in my own life and in the lives of people around me. When families are broken, it becomes harder for individuals to succeed, and the ripple effects are felt throughout society.

The Republican Party has always emphasized the importance

of family, and that's something that resonates deeply with me. I believe that family is the foundation of success—both personal and societal. When families are strong, children are more likely to succeed in school, to avoid crime, and to become productive members of society. When families are weak, the opposite is true.

That's why I support policies that strengthen families, whether it's promoting marriage, supporting parental rights, or encouraging community involvement. I believe that the government's role should be to empower families, not to replace them. And I believe that the best way to address many of the social problems we face—poverty, crime, addiction—starts with strengthening the family unit.

Faith and Politics

Faith has always played an important role in my life, and it's another reason I'm drawn to the Republican Party. As a person of faith, I believe that moral values and ethical principles should guide our decisions, both personally and politically. For me, faith isn't just something I practice on Sundays—it's a way of life. It informs how I treat others, how I make decisions, and how I view my role in society.

The Republican Party's emphasis on religious freedom and the protection of moral values resonates with me. I believe that faith should have a place in the public square, and I support policies that protect religious liberty. I also believe that faith communities play a vital role in addressing social issues, from poverty to addiction to education. Churches, mosques, and other faith-based organizations are often at the forefront of serving those in need, and I believe they should be supported in those efforts.

Moving Forward: The Future of the Republican Party

As I reflect on my journey as a Black Republican, I'm aware of the challenges that lie ahead—not just for me personally, but for the party as a whole. The Republican Party has a long history, and while that history includes many achievements, it also includes moments of failure and missteps. But I believe that the party's core values—freedom, personal responsibility, and opportunity—are still relevant today, and they are the values that will guide the party into the future.

I'm hopeful that the Republican Party will continue to evolve, becoming more inclusive and more reflective of the diverse voices that make up this country. I believe that there is room in the party for people of all backgrounds, races, and faiths. The Republican Party, at its best, is a party that stands for the individual's right to succeed, regardless of where they come from or what challenges they face.

As we move forward, I'm committed to being part of that evolution. I'm committed to advocating for policies that reflect the values I hold dear—policies that promote family, faith, and freedom. I'm committed to challenging the status quo and pushing for a Republican Party that is truly representative of all Americans. And I'm committed to standing by the principles that have guided me throughout my life.

Conclusion: Standing Firm in My Beliefs

My journey as a Republican has not been easy, but it has been rewarding. I've faced challenges, criticism, and even hostility for my political beliefs, but I've never wavered in my convictions. I stand by the decision I made at 18, when I registered as a Republican. I stand by the values that have guided me throughout my life: family, faith, personal responsibility, and freedom.

In the end, my political journey is about more than party affiliation. It's about standing up for what I believe is right, even when it's not popular. It's about choosing the road less traveled, and being willing to face the challenges that come with it. It's about honoring the legacy of my father, who taught me to stand firm in my beliefs, no matter what.

I am a Republican, not because it's easy, but because it's right for me. And I will continue to stand for the values that matter most—now and always.

Chapter Six: The 2024 Election—Most Peculiar Campaign In American History

As the 2024 election season unfolds, it feels different from any I've witnessed before. It's not just the stakes, which are always high in every election—it's the fundamental shift in the direction the country is about to take. For years, we've seen America pulled in opposing directions by political factions, but now, the tension has reached a breaking point. This isn't just about Republicans versus Democrats; it's about the kind of America we want to live in for the next generation.

Looking back on how we arrived here, it's clear that the 2024 election is more than a political contest—it's a referendum on the very soul of our nation. Will we choose a path that restores the strength, pride, and unity that defined America at its peak, or will we continue down a road of division, manipulation, and cultural upheaval? The campaigns of Donald Trump and Kamala Harris represent two vastly different futures. On one side, Trump embodies a movement dedicated to economic revival, strong national security, and putting America first.

On the other, Kamala Harris stands at the forefront of a progressive agenda that seeks to reshape the country through government intervention, identity politics, and increased social control.

The choice, this time, feels starker than ever. But as we navigate this critical juncture, it's crucial to understand how we got here—and how one political party, in particular, has manipulated and gaslit the American public, pushing us toward this moment of crisis.

The Rise of Kamala Harris: A Calculated Gamble by the Democrats

Kamala Harris' sudden emergence as the Democratic Party's candidate for president was not the result of democratic choice, but rather the culmination of a long-term strategy carefully orchestrated by party elites. When Joe Biden first announced his candidacy in 2020, he was presented as a steady hand, a figure who could calm the waters after the tumultuous Trump years. But it became clear early on that Biden's role was largely ceremonial. Behind the scenes, power was being consolidated in the hands of the party's more progressive wing, and Kamala Harris was always their candidate in waiting.

Joe Biden's decision to step aside for the 2024 race was not as surprising as it seemed. While his administration and the mainstream media tried to present him as fit and capable, anyone paying attention could see that Biden, in his 80s, was struggling with the demands of the office. His frequent gaffes, incoherent speeches, and public missteps were too obvious to ignore. Rather than risk a disastrous campaign that could expose Biden's frailties further, the Democratic Party quietly pushed him out, creating an opportunity for Kamala Harris to step in.

Harris' ascension wasn't a matter of public will but rather a decision made by the Democratic elites who control the party. From the beginning, the 2020 election wasn't about Joe Biden—it was about positioning Harris for this moment. As vice president, Harris played her role, staying mostly in the background, biding her time until the Democratic machine deemed the moment right to elevate her to the top of the ticket.

It's important to understand the full scope of Harris' career to see how she fits into the larger Democratic strategy. As California's attorney general, Harris built a reputation as a tough-on-crime prosecutor. But even then, she wasn't an ideologue—she was a political opportunist. She aligned herself with policies that were convenient for her ambitions, whether it was on law enforcement, immigration, or social justice. As she rose in national prominence, her positions shifted to fit the progressive agenda of the moment.

Harris' political agility is one of her defining characteristics. She doesn't hold strong principles that guide her decisions; instead, she moves with the political winds, aligning herself with whatever faction will offer her the most power. And now, as the Democratic Party's chosen candidate, she has fully embraced the far-left agenda that has come to define the party in recent years.

Her selection of Tim Walz, the governor of Minnesota, as her running mate was a calculated move to balance the ticket. Walz is portrayed as a moderate, someone who can appeal to the working-class voters in swing states like Michigan, Wisconsin, and Pennsylvania. But make no mistake—Walz is just another pawn in the Democrats' larger game. His moderate image is a smokescreen designed to lure in voters who might be wary of Harris' progressive platform. In reality, the Harris-Walz ticket is just another chapter in the Democratic Party's long-standing strategy of saying one thing and doing another. Behind their moderate rhetoric lies a far-left agenda that will continue to divide America, increase government control, and erode the freedoms that have defined this country for generations.

Kamala's Gaslighting Tactics: A Masterclass in Manipulation

Gaslighting is defined as manipulating someone into questioning their own reality, and in this election, the Democratic Party—under Kamala Harris—has turned it into an art form. The Democrats have been remarkably successful in shaping the narrative to make the American public doubt their own experiences and perceptions. They've created an alternate reality in which their failures are spun as triumphs, their radical policies are presented as common sense, and anyone who questions their agenda is painted as either ignorant or malicious.

Take the border crisis, for example. Under the Biden-Harris administration, we have seen record numbers of illegal immigrants crossing the southern border. The situation has spiraled out of control, and rather than addressing it, Harris has deflected responsibility at every turn. When asked about the issue, she has repeatedly downplayed the severity of the crisis, insisting that the border is "secure" despite overwhelming evidence to the contrary. In interviews and public speeches, she has blamed everyone but herself and the administration for the mess at the border, accusing Republicans of "fear-mongering" and "manufacturing a crisis."

This tactic of denial and deflection has become the hallmark of the Harris campaign. Whether it's inflation, crime, or the state of the economy, the Democrats have consistently gaslit the public into believing that the problems they are facing aren't real, or worse, that they're the result of Republican obstruction. They've created a false narrative in which their policies are always working, even when the results are disastrous.

When inflation began spiraling out of control under the Biden-Harris administration, Harris and her allies in the media tried to spin it as a temporary issue, claiming it was merely "transitory" and would soon be under control. But as months passed and prices continued to rise, the administration's story shifted. Rather than admitting to their failures, they tried to gaslight the public into believing that inflation wasn't as bad as it seemed, and that those who were complaining were either exaggerating or not understanding the complexities of the issue. Even now, as Americans struggle with the rising cost of food, housing, and gas, the Democrats insist that their economic policies are working.

This gaslighting has extended to every facet of the Harris

campaign. When parents began voicing concerns about radical gender ideology being introduced into schools, Harris and her surrogates painted them as intolerant bigots. Instead of acknowledging that parents have legitimate concerns about what their children are being taught, the Democrats dismissed them as reactionaries standing in the way of progress. Harris has repeatedly argued that anyone who opposes her vision for education is not just wrong but morally corrupt.

The manipulation doesn't stop with social issues, either. The Democrats have been remarkably adept at using the media to create an alternate reality in which their policies are always right, their opponents are always wrong, and any criticism of their agenda is rooted in ignorance or malice. They've managed to convince a significant portion of the population that the issues we face—rising crime, unchecked immigration, economic instability—are either not as bad as they seem or entirely the fault of Republican obstruction. This level of manipulation is unprecedented in modern American politics, and it has set the stage for one of the most consequential elections in our history.

Donald Trump's Comeback: A Movement Against Manipulation

In stark contrast to Kamala Harris, Donald Trump's return to the political stage isn't just about him—it's about a movement. Trump's campaign in 2024 is the continuation of a populist uprising that began in 2016, one that seeks to restore power to the people and challenge the elites who have controlled American politics for decades. The MAGA movement, for all the controversy it has stirred, is fundamentally about rejecting the manipulation, the gaslighting, and the elitism that have become the hallmarks of the Democratic Party under Harris.

The energy behind Trump's rallies is undeniable. His supporters aren't just backing a candidate—they're rallying behind a vision for America that puts their interests first. Trump represents a return to a time when America's working class was valued, when American interests were prioritized over global agendas, and when citizens felt pride in their country. In Trump, millions of Americans see a leader who isn't afraid to challenge the status quo, a leader who stands up to the elites and fights for the forgotten.

Trump's choice of J.D. Vance as his running mate only strengthens this message. Vance's story—rising from poverty to become a successful author and entrepreneur—resonates deeply with the working-class voters who form the backbone of the MAGA movement. He's not just another politician from the establishment—he's someone who understands the struggles of everyday Americans. Vance's presence on the ticket sends a clear message: Trump is doubling down on his commitment to the working class, to the people in states like Ohio, Pennsylvania, Michigan, and Wisconsin, who have felt left behind by the Democratic Party's shift toward coastal elites and progressive priorities. Vance's life story is a testament to the idea that the American Dream is still attainable for those willing to work hard, and together with Trump, they're offering a vision of an America that values personal responsibility, economic opportunity, and individual freedom.

But it's more than just rhetoric. Trump's 2024 campaign is not about empty slogans or pandering to the media. It's about delivering real, tangible results. Trump has a record of success to back up his promises. During his first term, he delivered on key economic issues: tax cuts, deregulation, and energy independence. Under his leadership, the economy surged, unemployment dropped to record lows, and wages for American workers grew for the first time in years. He made trade deals that put America first, renegotiating NAFTA and standing up to China's unfair trade practices.

These achievements resonate with voters because they were real. People saw the results in their paychecks, in the lowering of taxes, in the energy sector, and in the sense of pride they felt in being American again. This is in sharp contrast to the hollow promises made by the Biden-Harris administration, where the average American has seen little to no benefit from the so-called economic recovery.

The Democrats' Strategy: Divide and Conquer

One of the most disturbing tactics employed by the Democratic Party under Kamala Harris is their deliberate effort to divide the nation. Rather than focusing on policies that unite Americans around shared goals and values, Harris and her party have leaned into identity politics as a means to consolidate power. They have used race, gender, class, and cultural differences to pit Americans against one another, creating a landscape of constant social tension and unrest.

For years now, the Democrats have made it a point to emphasize division rather than unity. They've weaponized issues like race and gender identity, using them not as a way to foster understanding or inclusiveness, but as political tools to deepen divides. The promotion of critical race theory in schools, the constant framing of every issue through a racial lens, and the emphasis on "equity" over equality are all part of a strategy designed to fracture the American population.

Critical race theory, in particular, has been a flash point in this election. By promoting the idea that America is inherently racist and that its institutions are fundamentally unjust, the Democrats have sown distrust in the very fabric of the nation. They have convinced many young people that the American Dream is a lie, that the system is rigged against them, and that only through the radical transformation of society can justice be achieved. This is not just an academic debate—it's a deliberate political strategy aimed at breaking down the unity that once held this country together.

Kamala Harris has fully embraced this divisive rhetoric, often framing her campaign in terms of fighting against systemic racism and injustice. But instead of offering solutions that could heal and unify the country, she has doubled down on identity politics. Her speeches are filled with language about marginalized groups, oppressed populations, and the need to tear down the old structures of American life. But what does this actually achieve? It alienates large portions of the population, particularly working-class Americans who feel that they are being blamed for problems they had no hand in creating.

Harris' stance on gender identity is another example of how the Democrats have used cultural issues to drive a wedge between different segments of society. The radical push for gender identity education in schools has sparked outrage among parents across the country. It's not that people are against the rights of transgender individuals—far from it. Most Americans believe in the principle of live and let live. But the problem arises when this ideology is forced upon children at an early age, without the consent of parents, and when those who object are labeled as bigots.

This approach has polarized the country even further. The Democrats have cast anyone who questions their stance on gender identity as being on the wrong side of history, using the same tactic they've applied to race relations. They've framed it as a moral imperative, when in reality, it's just another political tool they're using to divide and conquer. By driving these cultural wedges between Americans, Harris and the Democrats have distracted the public from the real issues facing the country—economic stagnation, rising crime, and a crumbling education system.

Economic Illusions: The Reality of Harris' Agenda

If there's one area where the manipulation tactics of the Democratic Party are most apparent, it's in their handling of the economy. From the very beginning of the Biden-Harris administration, Americans were promised that massive government spending on infrastructure, green energy, and social programs would lead to widespread prosperity. But as we've seen, the reality has been quite different. Instead of the robust recovery that was promised, we've seen inflation spiral out of control, housing become more unaffordable, and wages fail to keep up with the rising cost of living.

Kamala Harris has repeatedly tried to spin the situation, claiming that the administration's policies are working and that the economic struggles of ordinary Americans are either exaggerated or the result of external forces. But for the millions of Americans who are struggling to make ends meet, these claims ring hollow. Inflation has hit the hardest in key areas like housing, food, and gas prices—essentials that no one can do without.

Harris has attempted to frame the rising cost of living as a temporary inconvenience that will soon be resolved, but this is simply another form of gaslighting. The average American family doesn't care about long-term projections or complicated economic theories—they care about being able to pay their rent, feed their families, and fill their gas tanks without breaking the bank. Harris and the Democrats, however, have consistently downplayed these concerns, instead touting their infrastructure plans and green energy investments as proof that their economic agenda is working.

But here's the truth: these investments are not helping the average American. The Democrats' green energy push, while appealing to progressive elites, has resulted in higher energy prices for everyone. By restricting the oil and gas industries, the Biden-Harris administration has made it harder and more expensive for Americans to heat their homes, drive their cars, and power their businesses. All of this has been done in the name of fighting climate change, but the reality is that these policies are hurting the very people Harris claims to represent.

Meanwhile, Trump's message on the economy is simple: put America first. He understands that the key to prosperity is not more government intervention, but less. His plan to lower taxes, deregulate industries, and unleash American energy independence resonates because it's grounded in common sense. Americans don't want handouts—they want jobs, opportunities, and a government that gets out of the way. Trump's economic message is clear: he will bring back the policies that worked during his first term—policies that created jobs, raised wages, and put more money in the pockets of American workers.

This contrast between Trump's plan for economic revival and Harris' empty promises couldn't be starker. While Harris and the Democrats focus on abstract concepts like equity and environmental justice, Trump is focused on real, tangible solutions to the problems Americans face every day. The American people don't want to be told what's good for them by a distant government—they want to be empowered to build their own success. That's what Trump represents, and that's why his message is resonating with so many.

Immigration: The Border Crisis the Democrats Created

One of the defining issues of the 2024 election is immigration, particularly the crisis at the southern border. Under the Biden-

Harris administration, the situation has reached a tipping point. Illegal border crossings have surged to record levels, overwhelming the system and creating chaos not only at the border but in cities across the country. Harris, who was famously put in charge of addressing the root causes of migration early in her tenure as vice president, has done little to resolve the situation. Instead, her response has been a mixture of deflection, denial, and empty rhetoric.

From day one, the Biden-Harris administration has taken a soft stance on immigration enforcement, signaling to the world that America's borders are open for business. This has resulted in a flood of migrants, many of whom are not just seeking asylum but are being trafficked by cartels and smugglers. The humanitarian crisis at the border is real, yet the Democrats have done their best to ignore it, hoping the media and public will move on to other issues.

Harris has repeatedly tried to frame the border crisis as a problem that was inherited from Trump, but this is just another example of her gaslighting tactics. The reality is that Trump's border policies were working. Under his administration, illegal immigration was at historic lows, thanks to his efforts to build the border wall, enforce immigration laws, and negotiate agreements with Mexico and Central American countries to curb the flow of migrants. Harris, however, has dismantled these policies, allowing the border crisis to spiral out of control.

The Democrats' ultimate goal here is clear—they see illegal immigration as a way to reshape the American electorate. By granting amnesty to millions of undocumented immigrants, the Democratic Party hopes to secure a permanent voting base that will keep them in power for generations to come. They're not interested in securing the border or upholding the rule of law—they're interested in importing voters and maintaining their grip on power.

Trump's message on immigration is simple: secure the border, enforce the law, and put American citizens first. He understands that a nation without borders is not a nation at all, and that unchecked immigration not only threatens national security but also strains public resources and drives down wages for American workers. Trump's commitment to finishing the border wall and implementing smart immigration policies is resonating with voters who are tired of the chaos and lawlessness that has characterized the Biden-Harris years.

Cultural Issues: The Fight for America's Values

Beyond the economy and immigration, this election is also about something much deeper—America's values. The cultural battles that have erupted over the past few years have placed the 2024 election at the center of a larger struggle over what kind of country America will become. These cultural issues—spanning from gender identity and race to education and the role of government in everyday life—are not just political talking points. They touch on the very foundation of what it means to be an American. And as we approach the election, the contrast between the two visions for America couldn't be clearer.

Kamala Harris and the Democrats have fully embraced what many call the "woke agenda." Their policies focus on radical social transformation—redefining gender, reinterpreting race relations, and challenging the traditional values that have been at the core of American identity for generations. They argue that America's institutions are inherently flawed, and only through progressive reforms can true justice and equality be achieved. While this rhetoric may appeal to the most progressive elements of the party, it has alienated millions of Americans who feel that these changes are being forced upon them without their consent or understanding.

One of the most contentious cultural issues is the Democrats' push for gender identity to be introduced in schools, often at very young ages. Kamala Harris has been a vocal supporter of policies that require schools to teach children about gender fluidity and allow them to choose their gender identities without parental involvement. For many parents, this feels like an overreach of government power into the most private aspects of family life. They believe that these decisions should be made within the family, not by schools or government officials.

The result has been a growing movement of concerned parents who are fighting back against these policies. Across the country, we've seen school board meetings erupt in protests as parents demand more control over their children's education. But instead of addressing these concerns, Harris and her allies have doubled down, accusing these parents of intolerance and bigotry. Once again, the Democrats have employed their gaslighting tactics, framing the debate as one between progress and backwardness, rather than listening to the legitimate concerns of everyday Americans.

This isn't just about gender identity, though. The same divisive tactics are being used in debates over race and critical race theory. The Democrats have pushed critical race theory into schools, workplaces, and even the military, arguing that America's history is one of systemic racism that continues to shape the country today. But what they fail to acknowledge is that critical race theory doesn't promote unity or understanding—it promotes division. It teaches children to see themselves primarily as members of racial groups, rather than as individuals with unique talents, abilities, and dreams.

Trump and his supporters have positioned themselves as defenders of traditional American values, standing in opposition to the "woke" agenda that seeks to reshape the country from the ground up. For many voters, this is one of the central issues of the 2024 election. It's not just about policies—it's about the cultural identity of America itself. Will we continue to embrace the principles that have made America the most prosperous, free, and innovative country in the world, or will we allow those values to be eroded in the name of progressiveness?

Law and Order: Safety vs. Reform

Another critical issue in this election is the question of law and order. Over the past few years, we've seen crime rates surge in major cities across the country, leading to a growing sense of unease among Americans. The defund-the-police movement, which gained traction during the 2020 protests, has led to the weakening of police departments in several Democrat-run cities. The result has been predictable: rising crime, especially in low-income and minority communities that suffer the most when police are defunded.

Kamala Harris and the Democrats have tried to walk a fine line on this issue. On the one hand, they've supported calls for police reform, often aligning themselves with the more radical elements of the progressive movement that demand the defunding or dismantling of police departments. On the other hand, they've tried to present themselves as defenders of public safety, aware that the rise in crime is a major concern for voters.

But their rhetoric doesn't match reality. Under the Biden-Harris administration, we've seen more talk about systemic reforms than about protecting law-abiding citizens. The Democrats have been more focused on criticizing the police than on addressing the root causes of crime or ensuring that communities are safe. The result has been a breakdown in public trust in law enforcement, particularly in the cities most affected by crime. Meanwhile, police officers are leaving their jobs in droves, feeling demoralized and unsupported by their political leaders.

Trump, in contrast, has made law and order a central part of his campaign. He's called for more funding for police departments, better training, and stricter enforcement of the law. He recognizes that public safety is one of the most basic responsibilities of government, and he's made it clear that under his administration, criminals will be held accountable. His message resonates with millions of Americans who are tired of the lawlessness that has taken root in cities across the country.

But Trump's approach isn't just about cracking down on crime—it's also about supporting the police. He's made it clear that while reform is necessary, defunding the police is not the answer. Instead, he's called for more resources to be directed toward law enforcement, including better training and improved community relations. This balanced approach has won him the support of many voters who believe in the need for both safety and accountability.

The stakes are high in this debate. As crime continues to rise, particularly in Democrat-run cities, voters will have to decide whether they want leaders who will prioritize safety or those who will continue to experiment with dangerous reforms that leave communities vulnerable.

Foreign Policy: Strength at Home and Abroad

While domestic issues are at the forefront of the 2024 election, foreign policy cannot be ignored. Under the Biden-Harris administration, America's position on the global stage has weakened. From the chaotic withdrawal from Afghanistan to the mishandling of relations with China and Russia, the Democrats have projected an image of indecision and weakness that has emboldened our adversaries.

Kamala Harris, as the Democratic nominee, has aligned herself with a foreign policy approach that emphasizes diplomacy and multilateralism. She's focused on strengthening international alliances and addressing global challenges like climate change. While these are admirable goals in theory, in practice, they have often led to a diminished of American strength and influence. Harris and the Democrats have been reluctant to confront China's growing aggression, preferring to engage in endless talks while China expands its influence in Asia and beyond.

Under the Biden-Harris administration, America's credibility has taken a significant hit. The disastrous withdrawal from Afghanistan, which resulted in the deaths of American service members and the abandonment of thousands of Afghan allies, was a major blow to our standing in the world. It signaled to both our friends and enemies that America was no longer a reliable partner. Harris, who was part of the administration that oversaw this debacle, has done little to restore America's reputation.

In contrast, Trump's foreign policy is based on strength. During his presidency, he made it clear that America would no longer be pushed around on the world stage. He stood up to China, renegotiated unfair trade deals, and forced NATO allies to contribute more to their own defense. His "America First" approach was often criticized by the media and political elites, but it resonated with ordinary Americans who wanted a president who would prioritize their interests.

Trump has been vocal in his criticism of Harris' foreign policy, particularly when it comes to China. He's argued that Harris would continue the weak and ineffective policies of the Biden administration, allowing China to further cement its position as America's primary global competitor. Trump's message is clear: America must be strong at home and abroad if it is to remain the leader of the free world.

Election Integrity: A Lingering Issue

One of the most controversial issues heading into the 2024 election is the question of election integrity. The 2020 election, which saw unprecedented levels of mail-in voting due to the COVID-19 pandemic, was marred by accusations of fraud and irregularities. While the media and the Democratic Party have consistently dismissed these concerns as conspiracy theories, millions of Americans continue to believe that something went wrong in 2020. This lack of trust in the electoral process has fueled Trump's campaign and remains a major issue in 2024.

Trump has made election integrity one of the cornerstones of his campaign, promising to implement reforms that will ensure every legal vote is counted and that fraudulent voting is prevented. He's called for voter ID laws, cleaning up voter rolls, and increasing oversight of mail-in ballots. Trump's argument is simple: without confidence in the electoral process, democracy cannot function.

Harris and the Democrats, on the other hand, have framed these measures as voter suppression tactics, particularly targeting minority and low-income voters. They've argued that Trump's push for voter ID laws and restrictions on mail-in voting is an attempt to disenfranchise millions of Americans. But this argument ignores the fact that most Americans, including many minority voters, support common-sense measures like voter ID. They understand that election integrity is essential to a functioning democracy.

The debate over election integrity cuts to the core of what it means to live in a free and fair society. If Americans lose faith in the electoral process, it undermines the very foundation of our system of government. Trump's focus on this issue has resonated with millions of voters who feel that their voices were not heard in 2020, and it's likely to be a deciding factor in the 2024 election.

Closing Thoughts: The Stakes of the 2024 Election

As we approach Election Day, the stakes of the 2024 election couldn't be higher. This isn't just a contest between two political parties or two candidates—it's a battle for the future of America. On one side, you have Kamala Harris and the Democratic Party, pushing an agenda of radical social transformation, government overreach, and divisive identity politics. On the other side, you have Donald Trump, representing a movement that seeks to restore America's strength, pride, and independence—an America where hard work, individual responsibility, and freedom are the cornerstones of society.

This election is not just about policies. It's about the very soul of the nation. Kamala Harris and her allies in the Democratic Party are betting on a vision of America that embraces bigger government, more control, and the erasure of the values that have defined this country for centuries. Their vision is one where identity politics, government intervention, and divisive rhetoric replace the principles of unity, freedom, and personal accountability.

In contrast, Donald Trump is offering a path that leads back to economic prosperity, national security, and a respect for the values that built America. His campaign represents more than just a return to traditional conservatism—it is a movement against the manipulation, the gaslighting, and the elite-driven agenda that has divided this country. Trump's vision is one where government gets out of the way and allows the American people to succeed on their own terms. It's a vision where borders are secure, law and order are restored, and Americans are free to live their lives without being dictated to by bureaucrats in Washington.

This election represents a true turning point. We can either continue down the path of division, weakness, and decline under Kamala Harris and the Democrats, or we can choose to restore America's greatness with Donald Trump. The future of our nation is in the hands of the voters, and the choice has never been clearer.

As Election Day approaches, I know where my vote lies. I believe in a future where America is strong—both at home and on the world stage. I believe in an America where freedom, prosperity, and opportunity are available to every citizen. And I believe in an America where government works for the people, not the other way around.

This election will determine whether we reclaim that vision or whether we allow it to slip away. For me, the choice is obvious. The future of America depends on it, and I choose Trump.

This isn't just about one election—it's about the kind of country we want to leave for our children and grandchildren. It's about preserving the principles that made America the greatest nation on Earth. And it's about ensuring that the American Dream remains alive for generations to come.

With this election, we're not just deciding the next president— we're deciding the future of our country. Let's choose wisely.

Chapter Seven: Understanding Donald Trump – A Retrospective Look at His Political Journey

I've known about Donald Trump for as long as I can remember. He wasn't just a business mogul or a reality TV star to me—he was a figure who always seemed to be in the spotlight, long before he ever entered politics. One of my earliest memories of Trump is tied to boxing. My cousin and I were huge fans of the sport, and Trump was deeply involved in hosting major fights in Atlantic City back in the 1980s. He was part of the sports and entertainment extravaganza of the time. I remember seeing him rubbing elbows with Black athletes and entertainers, long before it became commonplace for a wealthy white businessman to associate with prominent Black figures.

Even back then, Trump stood out to me because he wasn't afraid to be in spaces that most people in his position wouldn't dare to venture into. He wasn't shy about standing alongside Black men, in a time when racial divisions were still stark in

America. Over the years, this part of Trump's persona stuck with me. Whether people love him or hate him, it's hard to deny that Trump has always been a disruptor—someone who doesn't play by the usual rules.

The Trump I First Knew

As a kid, I didn't think too much about the deeper implications of Trump's presence in these spaces. But as I grew older and became more politically aware, I started paying closer attention to his business moves, his interviews, and his public persona. Trump wasn't just another billionaire. He was a man who built his brand on confidence, ambition, and an almost relentless pursuit of success. In many ways, Trump's approach to business and life reflected the values I admired—self-reliance, perseverance, and the belief that success is earned through hard work and smart decisions.

Over the years, Trump's name became synonymous with success, power, and luxury. His real estate empire, his hotels, and his television appearances made him a household name. But what fascinated me more than his wealth was his ability to negotiate deals, turn failing businesses around, and navigate the cutthroat world of real estate. Trump understood the art of the deal better than anyone, and his ability to strike agreements that benefited his interests—whether with business partners or foreign entities—showed that he was a man who thrived on high-stakes decision-making.

The Disruptor Enters Politics

When Donald Trump announced his candidacy for president in 2015, most people laughed. The idea that this brash businessman, who had spent his career in real estate and reality television, could seriously run for the highest office in the land seemed ludicrous to many. But Trump wasn't joking. He entered the political arena not as a politician, but as a disruptor—someone who was determined to shake up the system that he saw as corrupt, inefficient, and rigged against the average American.

What drew me to Trump's campaign was his message of change. For years, I had watched politicians from both parties make promises they couldn't keep. The Democratic Party, which claimed to represent the working class and minorities, often delivered little more than empty rhetoric. The Republican Party, while closer to my values, had become stale and out of touch with the realities facing everyday Americans. Trump was different. He didn't speak like a politician. He spoke like a man who was ready to take on the system, and he wasn't afraid to step on toes along the way.

His slogan, "Make America Great Again," wasn't just a catchphrase—it was a rallying cry for people who felt left behind by the political establishment. Trump understood that many Americans were frustrated with the status quo. He didn't try to be politically correct, and that's what made him stand out. He spoke directly to the people who had been ignored by Washington for too long, and he promised to put their interests first.

For me, Trump's candidacy represented something fundamentally different. He wasn't just another politician making empty promises. He was someone who was willing to challenge the entrenched powers in Washington and take action to deliver real results. His approach to politics—much like his approach to business—was focused on getting things done, not appeasing special interests or maintaining the status quo.

Trump's Business Acumen in Politics

One of the things that set Trump apart from other politicians was his business background. He wasn't a career politician who had spent decades climbing the ranks of the political establishment. He was a businessman, a deal maker, and that's how he approached politics. To Trump, running the country was like running a business. You had to be smart, strategic, and willing to take risks to get the best possible outcome.

As a businessman, Trump had spent his life negotiating deals— whether it was real estate developments, branding opportunities, or partnerships with foreign investors. He understood the art of negotiation better than most people in Washington, and that gave him an edge. He wasn't afraid to walk away from a bad deal, and he wasn't afraid to push back against people who were trying to take advantage of the United States.

One of the most significant examples of Trump's business acumen in politics was his renegotiation of trade deals. For years, politicians had signed trade agreements that favored other countries at the expense of American workers. Trump saw this and made it a priority to put America first in trade negotiations. His decision to pull the U.S. out of the Trans-Pacific Partnership (TPP) and renegotiate NAFTA into the United States-Mexico-Canada Agreement (USMCA) showed that he wasn't afraid to challenge the global order to benefit American interests.

Trump's approach to foreign policy was similarly influenced by his business mindset. He viewed international relationships as negotiations, where America was the client, and his job was to get the best possible deal. His decision to confront China on trade, impose tariffs, and demand that NATO allies pay their fair share were all moves that reflected his belief that America should no longer be taken advantage of on the world stage. He wasn't concerned with maintaining the status quo or appeasing global elites—he was focused on making sure America got what it deserved.

The So-Called Muslim Ban and National Security

As a Black Muslim man, I'm often asked how I can support a president who implemented what the media dubbed a "Muslim ban." The narrative pushed by Trump's critics was that his travel ban, which restricted entry from several predominantly Muslim countries, was an outright attack on Muslims. But when I took a closer look at the facts, it became clear to me that the ban wasn't about religion—it was about national security.

Trump's travel ban didn't target all Muslims, nor did it single out Islam as a religion. It was a temporary restriction on travel from countries that had been identified as high-risk due to their inability to properly vet travelers or their ties to terrorism. As someone who cares deeply about the safety and security of this country, I understood Trump's logic. His primary motivation was to protect American citizens from the threat of terrorism, and in his view, that required taking extreme measures to ensure that no one slipped through the cracks.

Was the travel ban controversial? Absolutely. But as I've learned in life, sometimes you have to make tough decisions that aren't always popular. In Trump's case, he was willing to take the heat from the media and his critics because he believed it was the right thing to do. He didn't want to risk a terrorist attack on American soil, and he wasn't willing to play political games with national security. To me, that showed real leadership. He was willing to put the safety of the American people above political correctness, and I respected that.

Trump and Race Relations: A Different Perspective

One of the most persistent accusations against Donald Trump is that he's a racist. It's a claim I've heard over and over again, especially when people see me—a Black man—wearing my "Trump Has My Vote Period!" t-shirt. But I always challenge people who make that accusation to point to specific examples of Trump's supposed racism. More often than not, they struggle to come up with anything concrete.

In fact, when I look at Trump's history, I see a man who has had positive relationships with Black people throughout his career. Long before he entered politics, Trump was rubbing shoulders with prominent Black athletes, entertainers, and business leaders. He wasn't afraid to associate with Black men in a time when it wasn't common for someone of his status to do so. Whether it was helping Mike Tyson get his boxing license back when others had written him off, donating to Jesse Jackson's Rainbow PUSH Coalition, or maintaining friendships with people like Herschel Walker and Jim Brown, Trump has always been willing to stand with Black Americans.

That's not to say Trump is perfect. He's blunt, brash, and often says things that rub people the wrong way. But I've never seen him as someone who harbors hatred toward people of color. To me, Trump is someone who values people based on their character and what they bring to the table, not the color of their skin. And that's something I can respect. I've never believed the media's narrative that Trump is a racist, and I'm confident that many of the people who make that accusation are simply repeating what they've been told, without looking at the facts.

Trump's Family Values and His Influence on His Children

When you look at Donald Trump's life, one of the most remarkable things is the influence he's had on his children. Trump isn't just a businessman or a politician—he's a father, and the way he's raised his children speaks volumes about the kind of man he is. Ivanka, Donald Jr., Eric, Tiffany, and Barron have all followed in their father's footsteps in one way or another, embracing the values he instilled in them from a young age:

hard work, resilience, and the belief that success is earned through determination and effort, not handed to you. Each of Trump's children has forged their own path, but they all share a common trait—they're driven, confident, and committed to their own personal success, much like their father. This speaks to Trump's values as a parent and the leadership he has provided within his own family.

Ivanka Trump: The Businesswoman and Advisor

Ivanka Trump is perhaps the most well-known of Donald's children, not only because of her position as a successful businesswoman but also because of her prominent role in her father's administration. As someone who started her career in fashion and later transitioned into the world of real estate and business, Ivanka's career trajectory mirrors her father's ambition and drive. She played a pivotal role in her father's business empire and later became a senior advisor during his presidency, focusing on issues like women's economic empowerment, workforce development, and child care reform.

What stands out about Ivanka is her ability to navigate both the business world and the political arena with grace and confidence. Her father's influence is evident in her no-nonsense approach to problem-solving and her commitment to getting results. Ivanka embodies the values that Donald Trump instilled in his children—work hard, seize opportunities, and don't be afraid to take risks.

Donald Trump Jr.: A Chip Off the Old Block

Donald Trump Jr., the eldest of Trump's children, is often seen as the most similar to his father in both personality and business acumen. Like his father, Don Jr. is outspoken, assertive, and unapologetically confident. He's taken on a leadership role within the Trump Organization and has become a prominent voice in conservative politics, often advocating for the values his father championed during his presidency.

What's clear about Don Jr. is that he shares his father's vision for America—one that prioritizes personal responsibility, economic opportunity, and national sovereignty. Whether it's speaking at political rallies or managing the family business, Don Jr. embodies the drive and determination that have defined the Trump family for generations. His close relationship with his father is evident in the way he approaches both business and politics, always striving to uphold the Trump legacy.

Eric Trump: The Quiet Force Behind the Scenes

Eric Trump, often seen as the quieter of the Trump siblings, has played a significant role in the Trump Organization alongside his brother Don Jr. While he may not be as outspoken as his father or brother, Eric's influence within the family business is undeniable. He's been instrumental in managing the Trump Organization's global portfolio of real estate, golf courses, and hotels, ensuring that the family's business interests continue to thrive.

What's interesting about Eric is that, despite his quieter public persona, he shares the same core values that have driven his father's success: hard work, discipline, and an unwavering commitment to excellence. Like his siblings, Eric has embraced the lessons his father taught him about leadership, and he has proven himself to be a competent and capable businessman in his own right.

Tiffany Trump: Carving Her Own Path

Tiffany Trump, the daughter of Donald Trump and actress Marla Maples, has taken a slightly different path from her siblings. After attending Georgetown Law School, Tiffany has largely stayed out of the political limelight, choosing instead to focus on her own career in law and public speaking. Despite her more private life, Tiffany remains a part of the Trump family's legacy, and her education and accomplishments reflect the same values of perseverance and hard work that her father instilled in all his children.

Tiffany's decision to pursue a career in law shows her desire to carve her own path, while still upholding the principles of success and determination that have defined her family. Though she may not be as publicly involved in the family business or politics, Tiffany's accomplishments speak to the strength of the Trump family bond and the influence her father has had on all his children.

Barron Trump: The Next Generation

As the youngest of Donald Trump's children, Barron has spent much of his life out of the public eye, but his father's influence is already evident. Growing up in a family that values hard work, self-reliance, and personal responsibility, Barron has a strong foundation upon which to build his future. While it's too early to say what path Barron will choose, it's clear that he has been raised in an environment where leadership and success are expected.

Donald Trump's approach to fatherhood has always been about leading by example. He instilled in his children the importance of ambition, hard work, and never backing down from a challenge. Trump has often said that he pushed his children to be the best versions of themselves, to always strive for greatness, and to never settle for mediocrity. This is evident in the way each of his children has pursued their own careers while upholding the Trump legacy of success.

Trump's Legacy and Family Ties

Trump's deep commitment to his family is a reflection of his broader values—values that emphasize strength, leadership, and an unrelenting pursuit of success. Just as he leads his family, Trump has sought to lead the country with the same principles. He views America as an extension of his family—something he's responsible for protecting, nurturing, and guiding toward greatness.

Throughout his presidency, Trump often spoke about the importance of securing a better future for the next generation, and that message resonated deeply with me. As a father and grandfather myself, I understand the weight of legacy. I know what it means to want to leave something better behind for your children and grandchildren. That's why I support Trump. He's a man who understands the stakes, both in business and in politics. He's spent his life working to build and protect his legacy, and that's exactly what he's trying to do for America.

Trump's ability to make deals, whether in business or politics, is central to his leadership style. He thrives on negotiation—on finding ways to strike the best possible deal for his interests. Whether he's dealing with business partners, foreign leaders, or political adversaries, Trump approaches every interaction with the mindset of a negotiator. He's always looking for leverage, always seeking to gain the upper hand, and always pushing for the best outcome.

That's one of the reasons I respect Trump so much. He understands that leadership isn't just about making speeches or appeasing people—it's about delivering results. In business, you don't survive unless you can negotiate effectively and get things done. Trump took that same approach to the presidency, and it's why he was able to accomplish so much in a short amount of time. He didn't waste time trying to win over everyone; he focused on getting results, whether that meant renegotiating trade deals, lowering taxes, or securing the border.

The Trump Legacy: Family and Country

For Donald Trump, family and country are deeply intertwined. His leadership style is a reflection of his role as a father—strong, decisive, and always focused on what's best for the future. He has built a legacy not only in business but also in politics, and that legacy will continue to shape America for years to come. His children are a testament to his influence, and their success is a reflection of the values he instilled in them.

Trump's presidency, like his business career, was about securing the best deal for America. He wasn't afraid to challenge the status quo, to push back against powerful interests, and to fight for what he believed was right. Whether negotiating peace deals in the Middle East or standing up to China on trade, Trump approached every situation with the same goal: to get the best possible outcome for America.

As I reflect on Trump's political journey, I see a man who understands the importance of family, of leadership, and of leaving a lasting legacy. He's a man who has built empires, both in business and in politics, and who has never been afraid to take on the toughest challenges. His love for his family is evident in everything he does, and that same love extends to his country.

For me, supporting Trump is about more than just politics—it's about supporting a man who shares my values, who understands the importance of leadership, and who is committed to leaving a better world for the next generation. Trump's legacy is one of strength, determination, and a relentless pursuit of success, and I'm proud to stand by him.

As I continue to lead my own family, I look to Trump's example of leadership—both in business and in politics. His journey has shown me that with hard work, perseverance, and a commitment to your values, anything is possible. And just as Trump has built a legacy for his family, I'm committed to building a legacy for mine—one that reflects the same principles of faith, family, and freedom that have guided me throughout my life.

The Donald J. Trump Journey Of Political Ties

Donald Trump's political affiliations throughout his life have been varied, reflecting both his evolving political beliefs and the shifting dynamics of American politics. Over the decades, Trump has changed his party registration multiple times, aligning with different parties for personal, business, and ideological reasons. Here's a detailed breakdown of his political affiliations, the years he switched parties, and the reasons behind those changes:

1. **Democratic Party** (Before 1987)

Affiliation: Trump was a registered Democrat for a significant portion of his early life, particularly during the 1980s. His family's real estate business was based in New York City, a predominantly Democratic stronghold, which likely influenced his political leanings at the time.

Reason for Affiliation: Trump's early years were marked by a focus on his business empire, and his alignment with the

Democratic Party may have been pragmatic. In New York City, where Democrats held significant political influence, Trump maintained close relationships with prominent Democratic figures, such as New York Governor Mario Cuomo and Mayor Ed Koch. He contributed to Democratic campaigns and forged political connections to facilitate his real estate ventures.

Why He Left: Trump began to express dissatisfaction with certain Democratic policies, particularly around taxes, regulation, and economic policy. He became increasingly critical of the Democratic Party's stance on issues like national security and government spending. As his personal wealth grew, Trump's priorities started to align more closely with the economic and business policies of the Republican Party.

2. **Republican Party** (1987–1999)

Affiliation: In 1987, Trump registered as a Republican for the first time. This marked his initial shift toward the conservative movement, though he remained a vocal critic of both parties when he felt they weren't aligned with his personal beliefs.

Reason for Affiliation: During the Reagan era, Trump admired Ronald Reagan's economic policies, which emphasized tax cuts, deregulation, and a pro-business agenda. Trump's belief in free-market capitalism and reducing government interference in business aligned more with the Republican Party. He also began to cultivate a public image that blended business and politics, even flirting with a potential presidential run as a Republican in the late 1980s.

Why He Left: By the late 1990s, Trump grew increasingly disillusioned with both political parties. The Republican Party at the time was deeply divided over social issues like abortion and the role of religion in politics. Trump, a New Yorker with more liberal views on social issues, distanced himself from the party's conservative base.

3. **Reform Party** (1999–2001)

Affiliation: In 1999, Trump briefly joined the Reform Party, founded by Ross Perot. This was a third-party movement that sought to offer an alternative to the two major parties, focusing on fiscal conservatism and reforming government processes.

Reason for Affiliation: Trump's decision to join the Reform Party was largely driven by his frustration with both the Democrats and Republicans, whom he saw as being too entrenched in the political establishment. The Reform Party, with its outsider appeal and focus on shaking up the system, resonated with Trump's brand of populism. Trump even launched a short-lived presidential exploratory committee under the Reform Party banner for the 2000 election.

Why He Left: The Reform Party quickly descended into factional infighting, with prominent figures like Pat Buchanan and Jesse Ventura vying for control. Trump saw the party as disorganized and not viable for a successful presidential run. He also disagreed with some of the extreme elements within the party, particularly Buchanan's socially conservative positions. Trump soon abandoned his 2000 presidential bid and left the party.

4. **Democratic Party** (2001–2009)

Affiliation: After his brief stint with the Reform Party, Trump re-registered as a Democrat in 2001. This shift came during the George W. Bush presidency, a period in which Trump was critical of the Iraq War and Bush's foreign policy decisions.

Reason for Affiliation: Trump's return to the Democratic Party likely reflected both his personal beliefs on certain social issues and his opposition to the Bush administration's foreign policies. During this time, Trump publicly supported Democratic candidates like John Kerry (2004) and Hillary Clinton. His close relationships with high-profile Democrats, including the Clintons, were also a factor.

Why He Left: As the 2008 financial crisis unfolded, Trump grew increasingly critical of both parties' handling of the economy. He also began to speak out more about issues like immigration and trade, where his views began to align more with Republican and populist sentiments. By the time Barack Obama was elected president in 2008, Trump was becoming more vocal about his dissatisfaction with Democratic policies, particularly on issues like healthcare (the Affordable Care Act) and taxes.

5. **Republican Party** (2009–2011)

Affiliation: In 2009, Trump switched back to the Republican Party as his views began to align more closely with conservative economic policies.

Reason for Affiliation: During the early years of Obama's presidency, Trump became increasingly vocal in his opposition to Democratic policies, particularly the Affordable Care Act (Obamacare) and Obama's handling of the economy. Trump's pro-business, anti-regulation stance, along with his growing focus on issues like illegal immigration and trade, brought him back into the Republican fold. He began to position himself as a critic of the establishment, both Democratic and Republican, which set the stage for his eventual presidential run.

Why He Left: Despite his affiliation with the Republican Party, Trump continued to criticize the political establishment on both sides of the aisle. His maverick, populist tendencies made him an outsider even within the GOP, and he briefly flirted with running as an independent once again.

6. **Independent** (2011–2012)

Affiliation: In 2011, Trump left the Republican Party and registered as an independent, fueling speculation about a possible independent presidential run.

Reason for Affiliation: Trump's departure from the Republican Party was part of his dissatisfaction with both parties, which he saw as corrupt and unable to address the concerns of ordinary Americans. He hinted at running as an independent, framing himself as a political outsider who could challenge the establishment.

Why He Left: By 2012, Trump had once again shifted his political calculations. He decided not to run as an independent, largely due to the difficulty of mounting a successful third-party candidacy in America's two-party system. He began to align more closely with the Republican Party as the party's base became more receptive to populist, anti-establishment messaging.

7. **Republican Party** (2012–Present)

Affiliation: Trump officially re-registered as a Republican in 2012, solidifying his ties to the party that would eventually carry him to the presidency.

Reason for Affiliation: In the years leading up to his 2016 presidential campaign, Trump embraced the Republican Party's economic policies, while simultaneously tapping into the growing populist, nationalist movement within the GOP. He positioned himself as a defender of American jobs, an opponent of illegal immigration, and a critic of trade deals like NAFTA, which resonated with many Republican voters.

2016 Presidential Run and Beyond: Trump's presidential campaign in 2016 was a masterclass in populist messaging. He ran on a platform of "America First," focusing on immigration reform, tax cuts, deregulation, and renegotiating trade deals. His unconventional campaign, which broke many of the norms of Republican politics, earned him the nomination and ultimately the presidency. Since taking office, Trump has continued to shape the Republican Party around his populist and nationalist agenda, becoming the most prominent figure in modern conservative politics.

Summary of Trump's Party Affiliations

1. Before 1987 – Democrat: Trump's early affiliation with the Democrats reflected his business interests in New York City and his connections with local Democratic politicians.

2. 1987–1999 – Republican: He switched to the Republican Party during the Reagan era, drawn to the GOP's pro-business, tax-cutting policies.

3. 1999–2001 – Reform Party: Trump briefly joined Ross Perot's Reform Party, running a short-lived presidential exploratory campaign.

4. 2001–2009 – Democrat: Trump re-registered as a Democrat during the Bush years, opposing the Iraq War and maintaining ties with Democratic politicians.

5. 2009–2011 – Republican: He returned to the GOP as he became more critical of Democratic policies, particularly those under Obama.

6. 2011–2012 – Independent: Trump briefly became an independent as he toyed with the idea of an independent presidential run.

7. 2012–Present – Republican: Trump returned to the GOP, ultimately running for and winning the presidency as a Republican in 2016.

Throughout his life, Trump's party affiliations have reflected his pragmatic approach to politics, aligning with the party that best suited his personal, business, and political interests at the time. His shift toward a populist, nationalist message has reshaped the modern Republican Party, making him a central figure in its current identity.

Although I didn't really join each religious sect or group, I made a point to immerse myself in deep research among them. I wanted to understand their teachings, philosophies, and how they aligned with my own principles. In my pursuit of knowledge, I explored Christianity, Judaism, Israelite's, Buddhism, and other spiritual movements. But even after all my exploration, I realized that you can't always fully commit to something just because it seems right on the surface. It took time to recognize that what you see on the outside isn't always what's happening on the inside. This discovery brought me to the realization that, despite my respect for all of these religions, my place was in Islam—a belief system that felt true to me after much reflection.

In much the same way, Donald Trump's political journey mirrored my spiritual exploration. Trump didn't just dive headfirst into one political party without understanding its core values. He switched affiliations multiple times, from the Democrats to the Republicans, even briefly exploring the Reform Party. Trump dug deep to find the political ideology that not only resonated with him personally but also empowered him to bring about the kind of change he envisioned for the country. Like my religious journey, Trump's political exploration was filled with periods of doubt, discovery, and reassessment. In the end, he found his home in the Republican Party, where he felt he could make the most significant impact, just as I found my spiritual path in Islam.

Sometimes, you learn that you can't fully give yourself to something just because you once felt drawn to it. Timing, circumstance, and the deeper meaning behind any belief system—whether religious or political—are critical to finding where you belong. Trump's journey led him to a place where he could align his vision with a party that best supported his goals for the American people. Similarly, my path led me back to Islam, but with a deeper understanding of why I am a Muslim— not because of the people but because of the faith itself.

There's a quote in Hadith that I've always held close: "Never follow Muslims; follow the Quran." In other words, don't follow people blindly—follow what you know is right. Trump exemplified this philosophy in his political decisions. He didn't align himself with parties just for the sake of doing so; he examined each one critically, weighing the principles that mattered most to him. Like my journey, it was about finding where he could do the most good for the people. And that's where the essence of leadership comes from—following the path that aligns with your values and allows you to serve others, regardless of the labels or affiliations attached to it.

Video Links:

https://youtube.com/shorts/MmV4cDS3Cfo?si=avGEWD6dJ9 n8rHHD

https://youtube.com/shorts/lbZGO4w6IDg?si=FvO7w27eCnV
d51LH

https://youtube.com/shorts/DVrd4MONCdg?si=8GEe3q4YvpR
1A1Aj

https://youtube.com/shorts/x9Uyem_NgBc?si=_3z79bpusWr
3qSMq

https://youtube.com/shorts/rozECTx6zOI?si=ZILTOcoNuVFs
gRca

https://youtube.com/shorts/U5FEyB1CQNg?si=v-EFPAkEac4v
Zf09

Chapter Eight: The T-Shirt – That Steadily Has Me Approached For Trump Talk & I Love It

It was an overcast day in downtown Atlanta, with the humid Southern air clinging to every step as I made my way through the bustling streets near the Georgia Aquarium. The sky was gray, the kind of heavy clouds that hinted at a storm yet left you guessing. I had parked a couple of blocks away from Ruth's Chris Steak House, the iconic Atlanta location nestled between the aquarium and the shimmering buildings of Centennial Olympic Park. It was a part of the city that always felt alive— tourists snapping pictures, street vendors selling their wares, and business people weaving in and out of the crowd with purpose. This part of Atlanta always gave me a sense of hustle, ambition, and grit.

But on this particular day, I wasn't here for a meal or to admire the city skyline. I was here for something much simpler, though no less significant: to grab a cup of coffee, take in the atmosphere, and wear my favorite shirt—my bold, black-and-white "TRUMP HAS MY VOTE PERIOD!" t-shirt.

I've worn this shirt countless times. It's soft and worn in the way that only your favorite shirts can be, with the lettering starting to fray ever so slightly at the edges from too many washes. But each time I wear it, especially in a city as politically diverse and charged as Atlanta, it's as if I'm walking around with a giant target on my back. Not for hostility, though sometimes that happens too, but for conversation. Today would be no different.

A Stroll through the Heart of Atlanta

The streets were alive with people from all walks of life. The aquarium was packed, as always, with families eager to show their kids the wonders of marine life. The lines outside of the nearby Coca-Cola Museum twisted and turned like a maze, while the sound of city buses and cars formed a constant hum in the background. Tourists crowded the sidewalks with cameras and smartphones, documenting their every step, and street musicians played soulful tunes that danced on the air.

I strolled past, walking casually, yet feeling the familiar sensation of eyes on me. In a place as public as downtown Atlanta, my shirt was more than just an item of clothing. It was a conversation starter, a challenge, and, for some, an outright provocation.

It didn't take long for the first interaction of the day. A young woman, likely in her mid-20s, with straight black hair pulled into a ponytail, stood at the edge of the park. She was wearing a baggy t-shirt and athletic shoes, a Georgia State University student, perhaps, by the look of her backpack.

"Excuse me," she said, approaching with a mixture of curiosity and apprehension in her voice. I knew what was coming. "Can I ask you something? Why would you wear a Trump shirt, especially as a Black man?"

This wasn't the first time I'd been asked this, and it certainly wouldn't be the last.

"Why not?" I responded with a calm smile. "What makes you think I wouldn't wear it?"

She hesitated, as if trying to find the right words. I could tell she was nervous about offending me, yet genuinely curious. "Well, you know, everything they say about him being racist... and misogynistic. I just don't understand why you would support someone like that."

Ah, the usual points. I leaned in slightly, my voice steady. "What makes you think he's racist?"

That's when the familiar look appeared—the one that says, You're Black. Don't you know? But I didn't stop there. I pressed on, enjoying the conversation for what it was—a chance to challenge someone's assumptions.

"Was Trump racist when he helped Mike Tyson get his boxing

license reinstated after everyone else blackballed him? Or maybe he was racist when he donated to Jesse Jackson's Rainbow PUSH Coalition, a civil rights organization focused on helping the underprivileged. What about Herschel Walker? Or Jim Brown, the Hall of Fame football player and civil rights activist who has openly called Trump a friend?"

Her brow furrowed. She didn't know what to say. This wasn't the narrative she had been fed. "Well, I mean, he's just... he seems like someone who takes advantage of people in his business deals."

Now it was my turn to smile knowingly. "Have you ever run a business?" I asked, my eyes meeting hers. She shook her head.

"Well, let me break it down for you. I've run a business. In fact, I've been in business for over twenty years. When you're at the top—when you've built something successful—everyone comes at you trying to take a piece of it. You have to be tough, you have to make hard decisions. The media loves to paint Trump as a man who takes advantage of people, but what about Nike? What about all those companies that produce their shoes in sweatshops overseas, paying kids pennies to make sneakers that they sell here for hundreds of dollars?" She looked down at her feet. She was wearing Nike sneakers.

I let that sit for a moment, watching the gears turn in her head. It wasn't about attacking her—far from it. I wanted her to think, to question what she had been told, just as I had done years before.

The Georgia Aquarium in the Distance

As we talked, the massive glass walls of the Georgia Aquarium loomed nearby. I could see children pressed up against the windows, marveling at the creatures swimming in the giant tanks. The scene was a reminder of innocence, of people's innate curiosity before their minds are shaped by the world around them. I couldn't help but think that the young woman in front of me was like one of those children—seeing the world through a narrow lens, but ready to have it expanded if given the chance.

She finally broke the silence. "I guess I never really thought about it like that. But still, what about the Muslim Ban? That seemed pretty harsh."

I nodded. "Yeah, I get that. As a Black Muslim man, I understand how it might have felt like an attack. But here's the thing—you have to understand the mindset behind the decision. Trump wasn't targeting Muslims because of their religion. He was trying to protect the country. The ban was on countries that had been identified as high-risk for terrorism. Was it fair to everyone? No. But his job as president was to protect America, just like you'd protect your own home. If there's even a small chance that something could go wrong, are you going to take that risk? Would you let someone into your home just because they happen to know a friend of yours?" She thought for a moment before answering. "I guess not."

"That's all Trump was doing," I continued. "He was trying to keep the country safe. You don't have to agree with everything

160

he does, but at least understand why he does it."

The Heart of Atlanta

Our conversation drifted, and she eventually thanked me for sharing my perspective. As she walked away, I looked around the vibrant cityscape of downtown Atlanta. The streets were bustling with life—the hum of the MARTA train overhead, the constant chatter of tourists, the occasional honk of a car in traffic. The city itself was a melting pot of cultures, people from all walks of life, coming together in a place where the past and present coexisted. From the historic civil rights landmarks scattered across the city to the modern marvels like the Georgia Aquarium and the shiny new high-rises, Atlanta was a city of contrasts—just like America.

I knew that wearing my "TRUMP HAS MY VOTE PERIOD!" shirt here was always going to spark conversations, and I welcomed them. To me, it wasn't about proving anyone wrong or winning an argument. It was about dialogue. It was about giving people the opportunity to see things from a different angle, just as I had years ago when I started researching Trump and his policies.

As I strolled past Ruth's Chris, the scent of sizzling steaks wafting through the air, I thought about the many times I'd had these kinds of conversations in this very area. Atlanta, with its deep political history and its role in the civil rights movement, was a city where people took their beliefs seriously. But it was also a place where, if you were willing to listen and engage, you could find common ground—even with those who started out on the opposite side.

A New Encounter, A New Perspective

Just as I reached the corner of the street, another man approached me—this time, an older gentleman, his graying hair slicked back and his suit slightly worn from years of use. He looked like someone who had seen it all—maybe a businessman, or a retired professional enjoying his time in the city.

"Nice shirt," he said with a chuckle. "I gotta ask—what made you decide to support Trump?"

I smiled, already knowing where this conversation was headed. "Let me tell you why," I began, and just like that, another conversation was sparked in the heart of downtown Atlanta. Each interaction was different, but they all shared one thing in common: the willingness to listen, to question, and to understand.

In a city as dynamic as Atlanta, where the past, present, and future collide in a symphony of voices and perspectives, wearing my Trump shirt was more than just a statement—it was an invitation to connect, to converse, and to find common ground in the most unexpected places. And that, to me, is the true essence of democracy.

The Unseen Roadblocks

The day after I completed and published my new website, trumphasmyvoteperiod.com, I was feeling a strange mix of excitement and exhaustion. It wasn't just the website—it was everything. Writing a book, building a platform, getting my ideas out into the world—all while being pressed for time. I knew I was rushing, cutting corners here and there to meet deadlines. But still, I thought, maybe a little support from my family and friends could give me that extra boost to keep going. Sometimes, just knowing that someone's got your back is all you need to refuel.

I decided to send the link to all my close family and friends, hoping for a few kind words of encouragement. A simple "Good job" or "Keep it up" would have been more than enough. But instead of the pat on the back I was hoping for, I got something that sent me spiraling in a completely different direction.

One of the first responses I got was from my eldest male cousin, my late father's first cousin. By all accounts, he's considered a leader among the men in the family, someone I always looked up to. I expected at least a neutral reaction from him, maybe even a little pride in what I had accomplished. After all, we're family.

When he saw that I was supporting Trump, his response wasn't anything close to what I expected. He texted back that he wouldn't even preview my website because, in his words, "I can't drive your car and mine at the same time." What? I was confused—completely thrown off by this metaphor. So I replied, "I'm not asking you to drive my car because you're not on my insurance." What I really meant was: I'm not asking you to take on my beliefs or drive this project for me—I just want your support.

In my head, I extended the analogy further. If I had just bought a new car—a Benz, for example—and I drove it over to his house to show it off, would he refuse to come outside and check it out just because he's a BMW man? That's how his reaction felt. It wasn't about the car; it was about me wanting him to be proud of something I'd accomplished. But instead, he wouldn't even look.

It hit me hard. Writing a book, creating a website, managing everything with no help—it's a lot. And in that moment, instead of feeling lifted up by family, I felt like he had taken the wind out of my sails. It's a shame when we can support total strangers more easily than our own family. I've always believed that if someone close to me worked hard on something, no matter what it was, I would show up, give them a pat on the back, and tell them I was proud. In fact, I'd go further. I'd offer any help I could to push them forward. But that's just how I roll.

The irony of the whole thing? This cousin is a staunch Democrat. He's so loyal to their agenda, but it's because of them that he's in the position he's in today. He should be enjoying his retirement after a successful career in finance. Instead, he's studying to get his CDL so he can make ends meet. The Democrats, the party he supports so fiercely, have wrecked the economy to the point where someone who worked hard his whole life now has to drive trucks just to get by in his later years.

It's baffling. Here he is, living the direct consequences of the Democratic policies he stands by, yet he doesn't see it. How can people be so blind? How can they live in the mess created by the very party they're loyal to and still not see the truth?

I shared the actual text exchange on my X account (@trumphasmyvote-period), for anyone who's curious to see the back-and-forth. But for me, it was another wake-up call. Sometimes, the ones you expect to be in your corner are the ones who throw the hardest punches.

That's life, I guess. You just have to keep driving your own car, no matter who refuses to look at it.

The Power of Our Vote

In the weeks leading up to the election, I've noticed something peculiar happening. A lot of people are being interviewed on the streets, sharing who they're voting for, and from the looks of these videos, support for Donald Trump is overwhelming. It's not just a random mix of folks either—it's working-class people, everyday Americans who've felt the weight of a broken system, and they know why they're casting their vote for Trump.

What's even more interesting is that when people are asked why they're voting for Kamala Harris, their responses—or lack thereof—are telling. The moment they're pressed about the policies they support, they're speechless. Not a word. Meanwhile, when you ask someone voting for Trump, they have no problem telling you exactly why: it's about the economy, supporting blue-collar workers, and refusing to send our money or troops to foreign conflicts that don't serve our interests. These people are vocal, informed, and they know what they stand for.

But something else caught my attention the other day. I overheard two Black women, both Democrats, talking casually about the election. What struck me was how dismissive they were of Black men. They weren't worried about us, as if our voices didn't matter, as if we wouldn't show up at the polls. It was like they acknowledged that many Black men are supporting Trump, but they felt confident that we wouldn't back it up with action. According to them, we're all mouth, no action.

That hit me hard. All mouth, no action? That's what they think of us? They don't believe we'll show up and make our voices count. It's almost as if they're betting on our silence. And I can't shake the fear that, if we're not careful, after the election, it might be revealed that they were right—that Black men talked about voting for Trump but didn't follow through.

This is a moment for us. A moment to prove them wrong. I implore all Black men who are saying they'll vote for Donald Trump—make your voice action. Don't just talk about it, be about it. This election is a chance for us to stand up for what's best for us and our families. It's more than just choosing a president—it's about taking a stand for ourselves, for our communities, and for the future we want to build.

To be thought of like this—disrespected, overlooked—it's a slap in the face. We've been taken lightly for too long. No more. This is the time to show our power, to make our voices heard. We must stand up for each other, support one another, and refuse to be silenced.

Let's prove them wrong. Let's shut them up. Let's make them take notice of the strength and unity of Black men in this election. Let's show them that our voices matter, that our votes count, and that we're not just talk. We're action.

We can rebuild our communities, uplift each other, and build value in a New Black America. The time is now. Let's vote Trump. Let's take back our power.

Where's the Fight for Our Children?

Now, I know what I'm about to say might get some backlash. My entire stance, really, is going to ruffle a lot of feathers, so why hold back now? For the past 18 months, I've been diving deep into political topics, focusing especially on education. I can't sit back and stay quiet anymore when I see what's happening to our kids. The system isn't educating them to prepare for life—it's confusing them. Instead of giving them the tools they'll need to benefit their families and society as adults, it's pushing an agenda that strips parents of their rights to guide their own children, their bloodline, their legacy.

I've seen enough to know something is wrong, and I've watched countless videos of board education meetings where people are standing up and raging against the system. Parents are angry, and rightfully so. They're standing in those meetings, calling out the government for taking away their right to parent, for forcing this twisted agenda on our children. But as I've watched these videos, there's something that stands out to me, and it's hard to ignore.

I've seen nearly every race and gender at these meetings, fathers and grandfathers, white women, Hispanic mothers, even Asian families stepping up to the mic. But where are the Black women? Yeah, go ahead and get defensive, but I'm telling the truth. Over the past 18 months, watching hundreds of videos, I hadn't seen a single Black woman standing up for the rights of her children in these education battles—until recently, when I saw one middle-aged Black woman speak out. One. That's it.

I found it strange, considering how vocal Black women are when it comes to fighting for abortion rights or emergency contraception. I've seen countless videos of them yelling in rage about their right to terminate a pregnancy, about the morning-after pill. So I have to ask—why is it more important to Black women to fight for the right to end a pregnancy than to stand up for the children who are already here?

Where is the participation in these battles against an agenda that's trying to confuse, control, and manipulate our children? Don't you care that your rights as parents are being taken away? That this system is pushing kids toward confusion, depression, and even irreversible surgeries? Or is it that standing up for your children just doesn't align with your own priorities? Is it easier to let the schools handle it so you can focus on your own life, your own choices, your own fun?

It's puzzling to me. I'm not trying to attack, but I have to question where the concern is. If you can fight so fiercely for your right to make decisions about your body, then where's the fight for the kids who need you right now? The system is trying to destroy our families, and our children are caught in the crossfire. Yet, there's silence from the very people who should be standing at the front lines for them.

If it's truly about protecting your rights, then what about the rights of these children to grow up without being influenced to go against their nature? What about their right to be guided by their own parents, not by a government with an agenda?

It's a bitter pill to swallow, but if you're not willing to fight for the children who are here, then maybe the priorities are all wrong. But hey, no one can tell you what to do with your body, or apparently, with your role as a parent either. Good to know.

SMDH.

Video Links:

https://youtube.com/shorts/0WJ49hV6OUE?si=bxleNeIH9SK
GBCF9

https://youtube.com/shorts/gKyHe6CpXB0?si=ZvptdEvNAEQ
orI9m

https://youtube.com/shorts/LPKk1r3313c?si=XOp___u8-IuTh
uiBH

https://youtube.com/shorts/kUhOnK4RBPE?si=rFdf65kvpMS
9dwwI

https://youtube.com/shorts/Pc4kXZfXToo?si=61l1EsqGrXhnw
CZ-

https://youtube.com/shorts/tm4Oa_276qA?si=Hq8J9335gE_
hpL-n

https://youtube.com/shorts/bhoQ_nKFOHc?si=YyHFmujGzq
_Gf-Oq

https://youtube.com/shorts/W2e9loGwTE8?si=v4S1h97FLVjX
Zcis

https://youtube.com/shorts/NlmA1r2jpI4?si=sqSHkXkFrrxRC
05F

Chapter Nine: The Kamala Harris Puzzle – Unraveling the Mystery of the Vice President

When Joe Biden selected Kamala Harris as his running mate, it felt like a political move that took many by surprise, myself included. In a field full of heavyweights, her rise to the national spotlight left many of us scratching our heads. Who was she really? How did she climb the political ladder so quickly, and what exactly was her appeal to the Biden campaign?

Sure, she was well-known in certain political circles, having served as a senator and as California's Attorney General, but to most of the country, Kamala Harris remained somewhat of an enigma. I decided to do what I always do when things don't add up—I dug deeper, determined to uncover the layers behind this complex figure.

Who Is Kamala Harris?

At first glance, Harris's background seems like a classic American success story. The daughter of immigrants—a Jamaican father and an Indian mother—who came to the United States with dreams of building a better life, Kamala grew up in a household that valued education and hard work. Her mother, Shyamala Gopalan, was a cancer researcher, and her father, Donald Harris, is an economics professor. By all accounts, she had a stable, middle-class upbringing that many immigrant families aspire to.

But as I looked deeper into her story, questions began to arise. There were inconsistencies in how she portrayed herself over the years, particularly when it came to her racial identity. In certain settings, Harris seemed to embrace her Black heritage, while in others, she leaned heavily into her Indian roots. It was as if she played both sides of the racial divide, switching between them depending on the audience she was addressing. This fluidity in her identity, while not uncommon for people of mixed race, felt calculated. It was almost as though she had learned to use her background as a tool, a way to present herself in the most politically advantageous light.

The Question of Identity

Kamala Harris's racial identity has been a subject of much debate, and for good reason. Some people question whether she is truly "Black enough" to represent African Americans, while others criticize her for playing up her Indian heritage only when it's convenient. The truth is, Kamala's identity has always been a complex and fluid thing, but the way she uses it raises some uncomfortable questions.

Why does it matter if Kamala Harris identifies more with one side of her heritage than the other? In an ideal world, it shouldn't matter at all. Yet, in today's political climate, where race is often used as a political weapon, Kamala's mixed background became a focal point during the 2020 election. Some African Americans were skeptical of her authenticity, questioning whether she could truly understand the Black experience, while others pointed out that she seemed to favor her Indian heritage—particularly in her earlier career.

To be fair, it's not uncommon for multiracial people to feel pulled between different aspects of their identity, but what struck me about Harris was how seamlessly she shifted between them. Growing up in a household influenced by both Jamaican and Indian cultures, she would naturally feel a connection to both. But the calculated way she seemed to present herself as either Black or Indian depending on the context made me wonder if she was using her background to pander to different groups. I couldn't help but ask myself: Does Kamala Harris really stand for all of these communities, or does she strategically use her identity to further her political career?

This isn't to say that she can't embrace both sides of her heritage. But as someone who values authenticity, I question the sincerity behind it. Was Kamala the Black candidate only when it suited her politically? Did she choose to highlight her Indian roots more heavily before her political rise to appeal to different segments of voters? These questions matter because in today's America, politicians' identities are scrutinized almost as much as their policies, and Kamala's shifting identity left me feeling uneasy about who she really is.

The Laugh That Confuses Us All

Then there's that laugh—the one that often seems out of place, the one that so many people, myself included, find puzzling. You know the one I'm talking about. It's that cackle that comes out whenever she's asked a tough question or when she's put on the spot. It feels like a nervous tick, something she developed to mask her discomfort when things get too heated or when she's struggling to come up with an answer. But is that really all it is? Or is there something more to it?

I began to wonder if this laugh was something she consciously developed over time. After all, Harris is a former prosecutor—a role where composure and control are critical. Perhaps the laugh is a defense mechanism, a way to buy herself a few seconds to gather her thoughts before responding to tough questions. Or maybe it's something more calculated—a deliberate tactic to throw people off, to make them second-guess themselves and lose their footing during a heated exchange.

Whatever the reason behind the laugh, it has become a hallmark of her public persona. Some see it as endearing, while others find it irritating or even disingenuous. For me, it's another piece of the puzzle that doesn't quite fit. It's as though Kamala is constantly performing, constantly trying to navigate the complexities of her public image, and the laugh is just one tool in her arsenal to deflect or distract when she feels cornered.

A Mysterious Political Ascent

Kamala's rise to the vice presidency still puzzles me. How did someone who was relatively unknown outside of California, and who performed poorly during the Democratic primaries, end up as Joe Biden's running mate? I've thought long and hard about this, and I keep coming back to the idea that Harris must have made powerful alliances early in her career. She must have shown the right people that she was willing to play the political game—a game that's not for the faint of heart.

Before becoming vice president, Kamala held a variety of positions, from District Attorney of San Francisco to Attorney General of California, and later, U.S. Senator. On paper, her career seems impressive, but when you look at her actual accomplishments, there's not much to write home about. Yes, she had some notable cases during her time as a prosecutor, but many of her decisions were controversial, particularly within the Black community. Her "tough on crime" stance, which included harsh penalties for minor offenses like truancy, disproportionately affected Black and Brown families. Yet, when she ran for president, she tried to paint herself as a progressive reformer, conveniently glossing over the parts of her career that didn't fit the narrative.

It's not unusual for politicians to reinvent themselves when they move up the ranks, but with Kamala, the reinvention feels forced, as if she's trying to play a role that doesn't come naturally to her. Her political ascent seems less about her qualifications and more about her ability to mold herself into whatever the Democratic Party needs her to be at any given moment.

The Biden Factor

When Joe Biden chose Kamala as his running mate, I expected a fierce competition within the Democratic Party for the VP slot. There were so many qualified candidates—candidates with more experience, better records, and stronger connections to key Democratic constituencies. So why did the other contenders bow out so quietly when Kamala stepped in?

I've wondered if the Democratic Party decided early on that Kamala was the safest bet. Maybe they believed that she could appeal to a broad range of voters—Black, Indian, women, and progressives—all at once. Perhaps they saw her as a candidate who could carry on the legacy of identity politics without alienating too many people. Or maybe they were simply desperate to beat Trump and thought that Kamala's selection would help solidify the diverse coalition they needed to win.

But here's the thing: in their eagerness to present a united front against Trump, the Democrats seemed willing to ignore the very principles they claim to stand for. The democratic process, which is supposed to be about giving people a choice, was sidelined in favor of political expediency. The party didn't hold a rigorous debate about who the best candidate for vice president was—they simply fell in line behind Biden's choice. And when Kamala stepped into the spotlight, the other candidates disappeared without a fight.

Was it because they didn't want to split the party, or was it something more sinister? Were they afraid of the backlash they might face if they challenged Kamala, a woman of color, for the nomination? In a party so focused on identity politics, it's hard not to wonder if the Democrats were more concerned about optics than about finding the best candidate for the job.

The Democrats' Ultimate Goal

At the end of the day, I can't shake the feeling that Kamala Harris is a pawn in a much larger game—a game that the Democrats are playing with the ultimate goal of defeating Trump and maintaining their hold on power. Her selection as vice president, and now her positioning as the heir apparent to Biden's presidency, feels less like a celebration of her qualifications and more like a calculated move to check off the right demographic boxes.

But what happens if she becomes president? Is Kamala Harris truly ready to lead the country, or is she simply a placeholder for the real power brokers behind the scenes? The Democrats have always been skilled at manipulating public perception, and I can't help but wonder if Kamala's rise is part of a broader strategy that has little to do with her ability to govern.

The Future with Kamala

If Kamala Harris becomes president, I have serious concerns about the direction of the country. Not because she's a woman of color, but because her track record suggests that she's more interested in playing the political game than in making real change. Her career has been marked by moments where she's chosen political expediency over principle, and I fear that as president, she would continue down that same path. If Kamala Harris becomes president, the question remains: will she govern based on her principles, or will she merely be the face of an agenda dictated by the Democratic establishment?

The Compromise Candidate

Kamala Harris represents a sort of compromise within the Democratic Party, a candidate that can appeal to various factions of the electorate but is not necessarily the first choice of any one group. Many progressive Democrats were not entirely sold on Harris during the primary; she was seen as too centrist and too willing to enforce policies that harmed marginalized communities during her tenure as a prosecutor. On the other hand, the centrist, establishment Democrats probably see her as too green, someone who can toe the line but needs direction from those who have been in the game longer. This lack of a clear identity makes her an ideal figure for the Democratic Party's leadership to mold as they see fit.

But what does this say about Kamala Harris herself? Is she truly a leader with her own vision, or is she merely a vehicle for the ambitions of others? Many voters have expressed doubts about whether Kamala has the necessary conviction to lead in moments of crisis. Her political record doesn't reveal a consistent philosophy or set of deeply held values—what it does reveal is an ability to adapt and shift positions when needed. In a sense, Kamala has been a chameleon, changing her political colors to suit the environment she's in.

While political adaptability can be seen as a strength, it also raises questions about authenticity. Can we trust a leader who has proven adept at saying what needs to be said, even when it contradicts previous positions? Does Kamala Harris have a core set of beliefs that will guide her if she ascends to the presidency, or will she continue to be a tool of the Democratic Party's larger goals?

The Laugh: A Mask or a Tool?

Then there's that laugh. By now, anyone who has watched Kamala Harris on the debate stage, during interviews, or in press conferences has noticed her distinctive laugh. It has often been criticized, labeled as awkward, disingenuous, or a nervous tic. But the more I think about it, the more I wonder whether this laugh is something more calculated than it appears.

For Harris, the laugh seems to surface in moments of discomfort, when she's caught off-guard by a difficult question or when she feels the heat of the spotlight pressing in. In those moments, the laugh acts as a kind of shield, a way to deflect and buy time. But is this something she's always done? Or is it a mechanism she developed during her rise in politics?

Imagine being Kamala Harris—half-Indian, half-Jamaican, growing up in a world where you are constantly navigating complex social and racial dynamics. Perhaps that laugh started as a way to lighten the mood in uncomfortable situations, to ease tension and prevent others from digging too deep. After all, being the daughter of two highly accomplished immigrant parents likely came with its own set of expectations and pressures. Kamala might have learned early on that a well-timed laugh could disarm potential critics and allow her to regain control of a conversation.

Or maybe the laugh is something she developed later in her career, consciously or subconsciously, as a tool to throw people off balance. In the world of politics, where every word is scrutinized and every gesture analyzed, the ability to control a room—even through something as subtle as a laugh—can be a powerful asset. Could it be that Kamala uses her laughter as a way to distract or confuse her opponents? To make them second-guess themselves, giving her just enough time to gather her wits and come back stronger?

Whatever the reason, the laugh has become a defining characteristic of Harris's public persona. It may be an authentic part of who she is, or it may be a carefully crafted tool that she wields when she needs to buy herself time. Either way, it's something that makes her stand out, for better or worse.

The Quiet Exit of Democratic Contenders

What also strikes me as odd about Kamala Harris's rise is the way other Democratic contenders quietly stepped aside when she was chosen as Biden's running mate. In any other election cycle, the battle for the vice-presidential slot would have been fierce. There were other candidates who had stronger resumes, more experience, and broader appeal. So why didn't we see a bigger fight from the likes of Elizabeth Warren, Cory Booker, or even Bernie Sanders? Why was the party so quick to rally behind Harris, despite her lackluster performance in the primaries?

The answer could lie in the Democrats' desperation to present a united front against Donald Trump. The party was, and still is, laser-focused on defeating Trump at all costs, and any internal division could have jeopardized that goal. Kamala, with her mixed-race background and experience as a prosecutor, ticked all the right boxes for the Democratic Party's identity politics. She could appeal to Black voters, women, progressives, and centrists all at once—or so the thinking went.

But there's another possibility—perhaps the party elites had long decided that Kamala was the future of the Democratic Party, and they made it clear to other contenders that any attempts to challenge her would be futile. It's no secret that the Democratic establishment wields immense power, often deciding behind closed doors who will rise and who will fall. Could it be that the party decided long before the 2020 election that Kamala would be their heir apparent, the candidate they would groom to take over once Biden's time in office was done?

Whatever the reason, the quiet exit of other Democratic contenders raises questions about the state of the party and its commitment to the democratic process. Was Kamala truly the best choice for vice president, or was she simply the most politically convenient option? And what does that say about the Democrats' willingness to sacrifice principle for the sake of political expediency?

The Future of the Democratic Party

As we look to the future, one thing is clear: Kamala Harris is being positioned as the next leader of the Democratic Party. Whether Biden serves one term or two, it's likely that Kamala will be the one to carry the torch once he steps down. But is she ready for the job?

There's no doubt that Kamala has the potential to be a powerful force in American politics. She's intelligent, ambitious, and knows how to navigate the political game. But the question remains: can she rise above the role of a puppet and become a true leader in her own right?

The Democratic Party's reliance on identity politics has worked in Kamala's favor so far, but it's also a double-edged sword. While her mixed-race background and status as a woman of color have undoubtedly helped her rise to the top, they have also left her vulnerable to accusations of being a token candidate. If Kamala wants to lead this country, she will need to prove that she's more than just a symbol—she will need to show that she has the vision, the leadership skills, and the conviction to guide the nation through its most pressing challenges.

Kamala's presidency, should it come to pass, will likely be

shaped by the same dynamics that have defined her career so far—political calculation, adaptability, and a willingness to play the game. But in a world where authenticity is becoming increasingly important to voters, Kamala will need to find a way to connect with the American people on a deeper level. She will need to move beyond the performative aspects of her identity and show that she's a leader who truly understands the struggles of everyday Americans.

Conclusion: The Kamala Harris Puzzle

As I reflect on Kamala Harris's journey, I'm left with more questions than answers. She remains a puzzle, a complex and often contradictory figure who has managed to rise to the highest levels of American politics without ever fully revealing who she really is. Her racial identity, her political record, and even her public persona seem to shift depending on the circumstances, leaving me—and many others—wondering what she truly stands for.

But one thing is certain: Kamala Harris is a force to be reckoned with. Whether she ascends to the presidency or continues to serve as vice president, she will play a central role in shaping the future of the Democratic Party and the country as a whole. The question is, will she rise to the occasion, or will she remain a puppet of the political machine that helped her get to where she is today?

In the end, the Kamala Harris puzzle is one that only time will solve. But as we move forward, it's important to keep

183

asking the tough questions, to challenge the narratives that are being fed to us, and to hold our leaders accountable—no matter who they are or where they come from. After all, that's what democracy is all about.

Video Links:

https://youtube.com/shorts/gt3qVzzA7gM?si=8vtE6UDeULxi Ps0m https://youtube.com/shorts/m7-6mDx6E9k?si=ehJQ18 yMjuEk4xGE https://youtu.be/kQe3_mkTqF8?si=kUUVVFUq9 JKJZZIz https://youtube.com/shorts/PsCQTvuzzPo?si=ExWgF YyroXWoF5Z https://youtube.com/shorts/G6VRJYdJRDE?si=H m_IO1y4Q1CHNANV https://youtube.com/shorts/DKqOUJkL4 eI?si=KelRfNszjL9HXWbc https://youtube.com/shorts/lf1IXn ug9Wo?si=z29RdZPFXFY-px2 https://youtube.com/shorts/ng pnqjmAeGk?si=stWTq3A-9Ptle77z

Chapter Ten: Key Policies That Matter to Americans

In today's America, certain policies have risen to the forefront of our collective consciousness. These issues are not just political talking points but real-life concerns that directly impact millions of lives across the country. Education, immigration, crime, healthcare, the economy, and deeply personal matters like abortion are pressing issues that we, as a society, must address with seriousness and depth. These are the matters that define our national identity, and the way we handle them will set the course for the future. This chapter delves into the key policy areas shaping our country today and explores potential paths forward.

1. *Children's Education and Transgender Issues*

One of the most fundamental concerns facing our nation is the state of children's education. It is no secret that the current system is failing our youth. Instead of preparing them for the future, we are teaching them to conform to outdated structures that no longer reflect the challenges of the modern world. Other nations are pulling ahead in terms of educational standards, and our children are being left behind. If we do not rethink our approach to education, America risks losing its competitive edge on the global stage.

At the heart of the problem is the length of the school year and the outdated curricula being taught. We need to extend school years and revamp the curriculum to focus on future-ready skills. Instead of simply teaching children to pass standardized tests, we need to equip them with the knowledge and abilities that will help them thrive in the real world. Financial literacy, community building, and technological education should be core components of the curriculum. Students must understand how to invest, plan for retirement, and contribute to the growth of their communities.

Moreover, children must be encouraged to pursue service-oriented careers such as becoming doctors, teachers, police officers, and firefighters. However, we should also teach them to be entrepreneurs and innovators, particularly in the areas of green technology and infrastructure. In the coming years, our society will need leaders who can develop sustainable solutions to environmental challenges and create self-sufficient communities capable of weathering economic and environmental crises. Our schools should be preparing students to lead this charge.

But education is not just about academics. It is about emotional and psychological development as well. Our schools should teach self-psychology and emotional intelligence. Students need to understand how to manage their emotions, particularly aggression and passive behaviors, in a productive way. Education must prepare students to face not only the professional challenges of life but also the personal, emotional, and social challenges they will encounter. Teaching togetherness, cooperation, and social responsibility is crucial if we want to build a progressive, unified society.

Unfortunately, the educational system has become entangled in the ideological debate over gender identity, which has led to confusion and division. Instead of focusing on academic excellence and emotional stability, schools have increasingly involved themselves in highly sensitive personal matters. Children, who are still figuring out their own identities, are being encouraged to make irreversible decisions regarding gender without the full involvement of their parents. This is not only inappropriate but dangerous.

Parents have the right and responsibility to guide their children through such deeply personal issues. Schools should not be stepping in to override parental guidance or pushing ideologies that children may not fully understand. We need to take a step back and refocus our education system on the things that matter most: academics, emotional well-being, and preparing students for real-world success.

Video Links:

https://youtube.com/shorts/mlIB-so8erE?si=J6KN9P64iNE4

VR4j

https://youtube.com/shorts/X-hPoIoiqy8?si=acC_k5BPpF9fd
Vwm

2. *The Economy: A Pressing Concern*

The state of the economy is arguably the most urgent issue facing Americans today. Across the country, people are feeling the
strain of rising costs, from gas prices to housing to groceries.
For many, it seems like the harder they work, the less they
can afford. Small businesses, the backbone of the American
economy, are being crushed by taxes, inflation, and increasing
operational expenses.

For the average worker, it feels like they are being taxed into
oblivion. By the time they have paid their taxes, bills, and living
expenses, they are left with only a fraction of their income.
In many cases, people are only able to keep 30-40% of what
they earn. This is simply unsustainable, and it is time for the
government to provide real relief to the American people.

One potential solution is to temporarily reduce taxes by 75%
for the next five years. This would give the American worker
some much-needed breathing room and allow businesses to
reinvest in themselves. By giving people the chance to recover
financially, the government can empower them to rebuild their
lives.

When people have more disposable income, they spend it—on

their homes, on their families, on their communities. This spending fuels economic growth, creates jobs, and drives innovation. By reducing taxes, we would also give small businesses the chance to thrive, which in turn would create more employment opportunities.

It is my belief that Donald Trump, should he return to office, could be the one to take this bold action. His understanding of the economy and his pro-business policies are what we need to get this country back on track. I would also encourage Trump to adopt the D.S.I.R. strategy (Dee-Sir), which focuses on strengthening America's infrastructure, promoting green technologies, and fostering innovation. The Democratic Party's approach to economic recovery has been slow and insufficient. We need bold, transformative policies that address the root causes of our financial struggles, not band-aid solutions that do little to alleviate the pressures people are feeling.

3. *War and Foreign Policy: The Need for a Shift*

For decades, the United States has been involved in foreign wars and conflicts, spending billions of dollars on military efforts abroad while neglecting the needs of its own citizens at home. While America has often played the role of the world's policeman, it is time to reassess our priorities. Why are we spending billions in places like Ukraine or Afghanistan when our infrastructure is crumbling, and our communities are suffering?

Our foreign policy should prioritize diplomacy and peaceful solutions whenever possible. But our first responsibility must be to the American people. We need to bring our focus back home and reinvest in our roads, bridges, schools, and hospitals. By redirecting our resources to domestic needs, we can create jobs, improve infrastructure, and ensure that our citizens have access to the services and opportunities they deserve.

The days of endless foreign wars need to come to an end. Our resources should be used to rebuild America, not to intervene in conflicts that do not directly affect our national security. This shift in focus is not just a matter of economics—it is a matter of national well-being. It is time to prioritize America's needs first.

4. *Social Security: A Broken System*

For millions of Americans, Social Security is failing. My father and uncle always told me, "Take your youth and make sure you take care of your old man." It wasn't until I got older that I fully understood what they meant. They were teaching me the importance of financial independence and planning for the future. Too many people work their entire lives, only to find that Social Security is not enough to support them in retirement.

The Social Security system, as it currently stands, is unsustainable. It leaves too many older adults struggling to make ends meet. After a lifetime of hard work, many find themselves in nursing homes, shelters, or worse, on the streets. Veterans, older women, and other vulnerable groups are falling through the cracks, and it is a disgrace to our nation.

We need to re-imagine Social Security in a way that provides meaningful support to those who need it most. I have spent 30 years working on a plan to address this issue, and my focus has been on supporting seniors, orphans, the homeless, veterans, and the hungry. These groups are often overlooked in policy discussions, but they are the ones most in need of our help. We need a new approach to Social Security—one that is sustainable, compassionate, and tailored to the needs of our most vulnerable citizens.

5. *Immigration and Border Security: Protecting America*

The crisis at the southern border represents one of the most significant threats to America's national security. For years, we have watched as illegal immigrants have poured into the country, overwhelming our border resources and bringing with them drugs, crime, and potential security threats. The situation has become so dire that it feels as though our border has been left unprotected by design.

I have long suspected that the Democrats are keeping the border open for political reasons. It seems as though they are welcoming new voters and shifting the demographic balance in their favor. But the consequences of this open-border policy go far beyond politics. Criminal organizations, drug cartels, and even potential terrorist cells are taking advantage of the chaos, and this is putting every American at risk.

If we are to secure the future of our nation, we must secure our borders. We need to stop the flow of illegal immigration and ensure that those who wish to come to this country do so legally. Technology—drones, robotics, and surveillance—can be used to protect the border, and lethal force should be considered when necessary to stop dangerous threats from entering. For children, robots can be deployed to apprehend them and return them to camps where they can be processed and sent back to their country of origin.

The current Democratic approach to immigration has failed. We need strong, decisive action to protect the future of our country and prevent drugs, crime, and national security threats from entering our communities.

Video Links:

https://youtube.com/shorts/_E_wT1FVnn8?si=Bo2PGrtE-wo jtUZY

https://youtube.com/shorts/EmcSvgM_NQc?si=2C3-WFount cCyp_p

6. *Crime and The Debate on Defunding the Police*

In recent years, the debate over policing has taken center stage in American politics. Viral videos of police brutality have sparked protests, and many have called for the defunding of police departments as a way to address these issues. But is defunding the police really the right solution?

There is no denying that police brutality exists, and that it has disproportionately affected Black and Latino communities. However, completely defunding the police would lead to chaos. Without law enforcement, crime would surge, and the most vulnerable members of society—women, children, and the elderly—would be left defenseless. The very people who need protection the most would be the ones to suffer if we dismantle our law enforcement systems.

Rather than defunding the police, we should focus on reform. We need a comprehensive overhaul of the way law enforcement operates in America. This means better training for officers, with a focus on de-escalation techniques, cultural sensitivity, and accountability. We need to ensure that police officers are equipped to handle the challenges they face in a way that minimizes harm and builds trust within the communities they serve.

Before the crack epidemic of the 1980s, police officers often walked the streets, engaging with the residents of their communities. They knew the people they were protecting, and this personal connection helped build a sense of mutual respect. Officers understood the difference between a young person making a bad decision and someone with serious criminal intent. They didn't jump straight to violence because they had taken the time to understand the community they served.

Today, that dynamic is missing. Many police officers are seen as outsiders—enforcers of the law rather than protectors of the community. This disconnect has only deepened the mistrust between law enforcement and the people. We need to get back to a model of community-based policing, where officers are integrated into the neighborhoods they serve and where trust is rebuilt through cooperation and mutual respect.

It's important to recognize that the police are not the enemy. The vast majority of officers are hardworking individuals who put their lives on the line every day to protect the public. But the few bad actors who engage in misconduct or abuse their power tarnish the reputation of the entire force. This is why accountability is so important. Officers who engage in wrongful conduct must be held responsible for their actions, and police departments must be transparent in their efforts to address these issues.

My own experience with corrupt police officers has shaped my views on this issue. When I was younger, I was involved in criminal activity, and I had several encounters with law enforcement that were less than honorable. In one instance, I was stopped by two detectives who unlawfully searched and assaulted me. Even though they found nothing incriminating, they returned later and robbed me of a PlayStation I had just purchased. This experience left me with a deep sense of mistrust toward law enforcement.

However, despite my negative experiences, I have never believed that defunding the police was the solution. Corrupt officers need to be rooted out, and police departments need to be held accountable, but dismantling law enforcement would create more problems than it would solve. The solution is to reform the system in a way that emphasizes transparency, accountability, and community engagement.

The reality is that without police, society would descend into chaos. Crime would run rampant, and people would no longer feel safe in their homes or neighborhoods. The most vulnerable members of society would be left to fend for themselves in a world where lawlessness prevails. That is not the kind of future I want for America.

7. *Drugs: A National Crisis*

The conversation around drug policy in America is often dominated by the debate over cannabis legalization. But while cannabis is certainly a topic worth discussing, it is far from the most pressing issue when it comes to drugs in this country. The real crisis lies in the widespread abuse of far more dangerous substances—opioids, fentanyl, crack, cocaine, and heroin. These drugs have devastated communities across America, leading to countless deaths, broken families, and a cycle of addiction that is incredibly difficult to break.

One of the biggest issues we face is that the legal drugs—prescription opioids, alcohol, and cigarettes—are often the deadliest. Tobacco kills nearly 500,000 people every year in the U.S., while alcohol-related deaths exceed 95,000 annually. Meanwhile, the opioid crisis, particularly the rise of fentanyl, is responsible for more than 80,000 overdose deaths each year. These legal substances, readily available in stores and through prescriptions, are far more dangerous than many illegal drugs.

The current trend in some countries to legalize all drugs is a dangerous one, in my opinion. I believe that America needs to first and foremost focus on securing our borders and stopping the flow of illegal drugs into the country. We need to employ advanced technology—drones, robotics, and surveillance tools—to monitor the borders and prevent the smuggling of drugs into the U.S. We cannot afford to be soft on this issue. Lethal force may be necessary to protect our country from the influx of dangerous substances.

Once we've secured our borders, we can turn our attention to helping those who are already struggling with addiction. Prescription drugs, especially those known to be highly addictive, need to be tightly regulated. They should only be available through government-controlled outlets, and we need to ensure that people have access to the support they need to break the cycle of addiction.

At the same time, we need to address the harm caused by legal substances like alcohol and cigarettes. These substances are doing immense damage to the health of our nation, yet they remain widely available and socially accepted. We need a public health approach that reduces the harm caused by these legal drugs and supports those struggling with addiction.

8. *Healthcare: A System in Crisis*

America's healthcare system is broken, and it's largely because of the unchecked power of insurance companies and pharmaceutical giants. For years, these industries have been allowed to manipulate the system to their advantage, driving up the cost of healthcare and medication while lining the pockets of politicians. As a result, Americans pay more for healthcare than any other developed nation, yet millions of people still cannot afford the care they need.

The only way to fix the healthcare system is for the government to step in and compete directly with the insurance and pharmaceutical companies. Just as T-Mobile disrupted the cell phone industry by offering affordable plans and forcing other companies to lower their prices, the government can offer low-cost healthcare options that will drive down prices across the board.

This isn't about abandoning capitalism. It's about creating competition that benefits the American people rather than the corporations that have been profiting off our health. By offering government-run healthcare options, we can provide affordable care to every American and force private companies to lower their prices in order to compete. The government needs to stop being beholden to these powerful industries and start fighting for the American people.

9. *Abortion: A Divisive Issue*

Abortion is one of the most divisive issues in American politics, and it's one that evokes strong emotions on both sides of the debate. Recently, I watched a YouTube video (https://youtube.com/shorts/VjXtHPX6jPQ?si=OzY4hiqreFAKABe1) where Kamala Harris blatantly misrepresented Donald Trump's stance on abortion in an attempt to manipulate her audience. This kind of dishonesty is not uncommon in politics, but it's particularly troubling when it comes to such a sensitive issue.

Trump has explained his views on abortion in detail, and his position is rooted in the importance of families and the belief that children are the future of any nation. His stance is not about controlling women's bodies—it's about preserving the foundation of society. But Democrats have seized on this issue as a way to scare voters, particularly women and people of color, into supporting their agenda.

Too many people are quick to throw around phrases like "Roe v. Wade" without truly understanding the legal nuances of the case or its successor, Dobbs v. Jackson Women's Health Organization. Roe v. Wade legalized abortion but included specific stipulations about the timing of pregnancies, while Dobbs overturned that decision and returned the power to regulate abortion to the states.

Neither case makes abortion illegal nationwide. It simply allows individual states to set their own laws based on the beliefs of their constituents. If a state's laws don't align with a person's values, they have the right to move to a state that does. It's a matter of personal choice, much like changing the channel on a television show you don't like.

As a Muslim, I don't personally believe in abortion except in certain circumstances. However, I also believe that each individual has the right to make their own decisions about their bodies and their lives. The government should not be dictating such personal choices. Religion and spirituality are deeply personal, and while I live according to my faith, I do not believe in imposing those beliefs on others.

The abortion debate has become a political football, and both sides need to take a step back and recognize that this is a deeply personal issue for many women. Men can hold opinions on the subject, but at the end of the day, it is women who are most affected by these laws. The conversation around abortion should be led by women, for women, and it should focus on finding common ground rather than stoking division.

Conclusion

In this chapter, I have outlined my views on some of the most pressing issues facing America today. These policies are not just political talking points—they are real-life concerns that affect the lives of millions of people across the country. From education and healthcare to crime and immigration, these issues shape the future of our nation.

We need leaders who are willing to tackle these challenges head-on with honesty, integrity, and bold action. The path forward is not easy, but it is necessary if we are to build a stronger, more united America. The policies I have outlined in this chapter reflect my belief in personal responsibility, individual freedom, and the need for a government that works for the people, not against them.

It is time for us, as a nation, to rise above the political games-manship and focus on what truly matters: the well-being of the American people. Together, we can confront these challenges and build a brighter future for all.

Chapter Eleven: Trump's Second Term: A Bold Economic Strategy to Revitalize America

Mr. President,

As the 2024 Presidential Election approaches, America stands at a critical juncture. The challenges before us—economic instability, outdated infrastructure, and the global shift toward renewable energy—require more than just incremental changes. They require bold, visionary leadership capable of transforming our nation and securing its prosperity for future generations. I believe that under your leadership, with the right plan and the right partnerships, we can rise to these challenges and emerge stronger than ever.

The plan I'm presenting today is called D'Allen's Security, Infrastructure, and Renewable Energy Initiative, or D.S.I.R. It's a strategic, comprehensive blueprint for modernizing the American economy, revitalizing our infrastructure, and positioning the U.S. as a global leader in renewable energy. But this isn't just about policy—it's about partnership. To make this vision a reality, I propose joining forces with one of the most innovative minds of our time: Elon Musk. Together, you and Musk could lead America into a new era of economic strength, energy independence, and technological leadership, while countering the rising influence of BRICS on the global stage.

Backing the U.S. Dollar with 10% of the U.S. Energy Reserve

The first pillar of D.S.I.R. addresses a looming threat: the stability of the U.S. dollar. As the BRICS nations—Brazil, Russia, India, China, and South Africa—work to establish an alternative financial system and DE-dollarize their economies, the dominance of the U.S. dollar in global trade is increasingly at risk. We must act swiftly to counter this threat and secure the dollar's status as the world's leading reserve currency.

My solution is groundbreaking: back the U.S. dollar with 10% of the nation's energy reserves. This strategy ties the value of the dollar to one of the most valuable commodities on the planet— energy. By linking the dollar to our vast energy reserves, we can create an asset-backed currency that not only provides stability but also instills confidence in global markets.

Energy is the backbone of modern civilization, and its role in the global economy cannot be overstated. Whether it's oil, natural gas, or emerging renewable sources like solar and wind, energy powers everything from transportation and industry to agriculture and technology. By backing the dollar with a tangible resource like energy, we would send a clear signal to the world: the U.S. dollar is not just a symbol of trust but is underpinned by a resource essential to the functioning of the global economy.

Furthermore, this move would provide insulation against inflation and economic volatility. Energy markets, while subject to fluctuations, are less prone to the kinds of sudden, catastrophic crashes that we've seen in other sectors. By using a portion of our energy reserves to back the dollar, we ensure that the U.S. remains the leader of the global financial system, even as other nations attempt to challenge our position.

In doing so, we would also deter other countries from aligning with BRICS or pursuing alternative currency systems. The U.S. dollar would remain the safest, most reliable currency in the world—its value tied not just to faith in American institutions but to real, tangible energy resources.

Creating U.S. Treasury Bonds Tied to Cryptocurrency for Infrastructure Revamp (10%)

The second pillar of D.S.I.R. is centered on modernizing America's crumbling infrastructure. To finance this ambitious initiative, I propose the creation of U.S. Treasury bonds tied to cryptocurrency, backed by 10% of the U.S. Energy Reserve. This innovative financial tool would bridge the gap between traditional investors and the rapidly growing digital economy, unlocking billions in investment capital for infrastructure projects that are vital to our nation's future.

One of the key infrastructure projects D.S.I.R. would prioritize is the development of battery-swapping stations for electric vehicles (EVs). This represents a major advancement in the way we think about transportation and energy consumption. Imagine stations across the country that resemble oil-change shops, where robotic arms remove a portion of the EV's battery pack, replace it with a fully charged one, and send the vehicle on its way—all in a matter of minutes. This system would eliminate the need for long charging times, making EVs far more convenient for everyday use.

Battery-swapping stations would also allow for regular diagnostics of the batteries being swapped out. This ensures that only optimal batteries remain in circulation, enhancing the performance and safety of EVs across the board. By reducing battery waste and maximizing their lifespan, we could lower production costs and increase sustainability.

In addition to revolutionizing transportation, D.S.I.R. would re imagine America's road infrastructure. Drawing inspiration from countries like the Netherlands and China, where smart roads are already in use, we would build roads that generate their own energy. These smart roads, embedded with solar panels and wind turbines, would harness the energy generated by vehicles driving on them, feeding clean energy back into local grids to power homes and businesses. It's a visionary approach that not only modernizes our transportation networks but also helps us meet our renewable energy goals.

The construction of these smart roads and battery-swapping stations would create thousands of jobs across the country, from manufacturing to technology development to maintenance. These aren't just short-term construction jobs—they're long-term positions that will help drive economic growth and technological innovation for decades to come.

Investing in National Renewable Energy Projects (10%)

The final 10% of the U.S. Energy Reserve should be invested in national renewable energy projects. This is where D.S.I.R. can make the boldest move, positioning the United States as the global leader in renewable energy. We must transition away from fossil fuels and build a clean energy infrastructure capable of sustaining our economy in the 21st century.

One of the most exciting opportunities is solar sidewalks. By embedding solar panels in the very sidewalks of our cities, we can generate clean energy from spaces that are otherwise unused. These solar sidewalks would feed energy back into the grid, powering homes and businesses while reducing our dependence on traditional energy sources. In addition to solar sidewalks, we can deploy rooftop solar panels on commercial and residential buildings, turning urban rooftops into power generators.

Another groundbreaking area of investment is waste-to-energy technology. By converting municipal waste into usable energy, we can address two problems at once: the growing waste management crisis and the need for renewable energy sources. Modern waste-to-energy plants can convert trash into electricity, reducing the amount of waste that ends up in landfills and providing a new source of clean power for communities across the country.

Investing in these renewable energy projects would create millions of new jobs in the rapidly growing green energy sector. From engineers and scientists to construction workers and maintenance crews, the renewable energy industry offers countless opportunities for high-quality, long-term employment. At the same time, it would reduce our carbon footprint and help combat climate change, leaving a cleaner, healthier planet for future generations.

Elon Musk: The Key Partner for D.S.I.R.

No one is more qualified to help execute this bold vision than Elon Musk. As the CEO of Tesla and SpaceX, Musk has proven himself to be one of the most innovative and forward-thinking minds of our time. His work in electric vehicles, renewable energy, and space exploration has already revolutionized multiple industries, and he is uniquely positioned to help lead the implementation of D.S.I.R.

Tesla's expertise in electric vehicles makes it the ideal partner for developing the nationwide network of battery-swapping stations. Tesla has already pioneered advances in battery technology and automation, and the company's experience in robotics would be invaluable in designing the systems needed for quick, efficient battery swaps.

Beyond electric vehicles, Musk's leadership in solar energy

through Tesla's SolarCity division would accelerate the deployment of solar sidewalks, rooftop solar panels, and other renewable energy technologies across the country. His commitment to sustainable energy aligns perfectly with the goals of D.S.I.R., and his ability to rally public support for innovative projects would help build the momentum needed to bring this vision to life.

But perhaps most importantly, Musk's proven track record of turning bold ideas into reality is exactly what D.S.I.R. needs. Whether it's launching reusable rockets into space or building a global network of electric vehicle charging stations, Musk has shown time and time again that he can deliver on ambitious projects. His involvement in D.S.I.R. would inspire confidence in both private investors and the American public, ensuring the initiative's success.

D.S.I.R. as a Counter to the BRICS Threat

D.S.I.R. isn't just a strategy for economic growth—it's also a powerful countermeasure to the growing influence of BRICS. As the BRICS nations continue to develop alternative financial systems and explore the creation of a unified currency, the U.S. must take decisive action to maintain its dominance in global trade and finance.

By backing the dollar with energy reserves, we send a clear message to the world: the U.S. dollar is the most secure, stable, and reliable currency on the planet. No alternative currency system can compete with a dollar backed by one of the most valuable commodities on Earth. This move would effectively neutralize any attempts by BRICS to challenge the dollar's status as the global reserve currency.

In addition, by investing in advanced infrastructure and renewable energy, we would position the U.S. as a leader in industries that will define the future. While BRICS nations may attempt to compete with the U.S. economically, D.S.I.R. ensures that America remains at the forefront of innovation, technology, and sustainability.

Economic, Employment, and Environmental Benefits

The economic, employment, and environmental benefits of D.S.I.R. are monumental. By stabilizing the U.S. dollar with energy reserves, we ensure long-term financial security for our nation. By modernizing our infrastructure with battery-swapping stations and smart roads, we create millions of new jobs and reduce our carbon footprint. And by investing in renewable energy projects, we accelerate the transition to a cleaner, more sustainable economy that benefits not only the environment but the health and well-being of every American.

Economic Benefits

The economic impact of D.S.I.R. would be transformative. By using a portion of our energy reserves to back the U.S. dollar, we would create a stable, asset-backed currency that instills confidence in investors, both domestically and internationally.

This move would not only protect the dollar from inflation and economic shocks but also restore its dominance in the global economy, countering the emerging threats from BRICS nations.

The creation of U.S. Treasury bonds tied to cryptocurrency would attract a new wave of investment, bridging the gap between traditional financial markets and the rapidly growing digital economy. This innovative financial tool would help fund the modernization of America's infrastructure, including the development of smart roads and EV battery-swapping stations, while also creating an additional source of revenue for the government. As a result, we could reduce the national debt, lower taxes, and stimulate economic growth—all without compromising our long-term financial stability.

Investing in renewable energy projects would have a similarly profound economic impact. As we transition away from fossil fuels and embrace cleaner, more sustainable energy sources, we would not only reduce our reliance on foreign oil but also lower energy costs for consumers and businesses alike. This would free up billions of dollars in disposable income, boosting consumer spending and driving economic growth across a wide range of industries.

In addition, D.S.I.R.'s focus on renewable energy would position the U.S. as a global leader in the green energy sector, attracting private investment and spurring the development of new technologies. The U.S. could become the world's top exporter of renewable energy technologies, further enhancing our economic power and influence on the global stage.

Employment Benefits

D.S.I.R. would also have a dramatic impact on employment, creating millions of high-quality, long-term jobs across multiple sectors. The construction of EV battery-swapping stations, smart roads, solar sidewalks, and waste-to-energy plants would require a massive workforce, providing jobs for engineers, construction workers, maintenance crews, and technology developers. These jobs would not only stimulate local economies but also help reduce unemployment rates in struggling communities.

Moreover, the renewable energy sector would offer countless opportunities for future-proof careers in engineering, manufacturing, and research and development. As demand for clean energy continues to grow, so too will the need for skilled workers to design, build, and maintain the infrastructure needed to support it. This represents a tremendous opportunity to retrain and reskill workers displaced by the decline of traditional industries, ensuring that they remain active participants in the economy.

In addition to creating new jobs, D.S.I.R. would also strengthen America's small business ecosystem. Entrepreneurs and innovators would have the opportunity to develop new products and services related to renewable energy, electric vehicles, and smart infrastructure, spurring economic growth at the grassroots level. This would not only diversify the American economy but also create a more resilient, competitive marketplace that fosters innovation and rewards hard work.

Environmental Benefits

Perhaps one of the most significant benefits of D.S.I.R. is its potential to drastically reduce America's carbon footprint. By investing in renewable energy projects like solar sidewalks, rooftop solar panels, and waste-to-energy technologies, we could reduce greenhouse gas emissions and mitigate the effects of climate change.

Smart roads, for example, would generate clean energy as vehicles travel on them, feeding that energy back into the grid to power homes and businesses. This would not only reduce our reliance on fossil fuels but also lower energy costs for consumers, contributing to a cleaner, more sustainable future. Meanwhile, battery-swapping stations would promote the widespread adoption of electric vehicles, reducing emissions from the transportation sector, which is one of the largest contributors to air pollution.

Waste-to-energy plants would offer another way to address both the waste management crisis and the need for renewable energy. By converting municipal waste into electricity, we could reduce the amount of garbage that ends up in landfills while simultaneously generating clean power for local communities. This would have a positive impact on public health, reducing the harmful pollutants associated with landfills and incineration.

In addition to these tangible environmental benefits, D.S.I.R. would help position America as a global leader in the fight against climate change. By investing in renewable energy technologies and infrastructure, we would set an example for other nations to follow, encouraging them to adopt similar measures to reduce their own carbon footprints. This would not only improve the health of our planet but also enhance America's standing in international climate negotiations, giving us greater influence over the future of global environmental policy.

Elon Musk: A Visionary Partner

To fully realize the potential of D.S.I.R., the partnership between you, Mr. Trump, and Elon Musk would be pivotal. Musk's track record as a visionary entrepreneur and innovator makes him the ideal partner to spearhead many of the initiatives proposed in this plan. His leadership at Tesla, SpaceX, and SolarCity has demonstrated his ability to take on seemingly impossible challenges and turn them into reality.

Tesla's expertise in battery technology and electric vehicles would be invaluable in developing the national network of battery-swapping stations. Musk's deep understanding of renewable energy and his leadership in solar energy technology would also accelerate the deployment of solar sidewalks, rooftop solar panels, and other clean energy solutions.

Moreover, Musk's influence as a public figure cannot be overstated. His ability to inspire and rally public support for innovative projects would be crucial in ensuring the success of D.S.I.R. With Musk by your side, Mr. President, you could generate the momentum needed to bring this bold vision to life, attracting private investment and gaining widespread public approval.

Together, you and Musk could transform the American economy, create millions of jobs, and lead the world in the fight against climate change. This partnership would be a testament to the power of collaboration between government and the private sector in driving innovation and progress.

D.S.I.R. as a National Security Strategy

D.S.I.R. isn't just an economic and environmental plan—it's also a national security strategy. As the world shifts toward renewable energy, America must reduce its dependence on foreign oil and fossil fuels to ensure its long-term security. The BRICS nations, particularly China and Russia, are making aggressive moves to challenge U.S. dominance in global energy markets, and we must act swiftly to counter their influence.

By investing in renewable energy and modernizing our infrastructure, we would strengthen America's energy independence, reducing our reliance on foreign energy sources. This would insulate us from the geopolitical tensions that often arise in oil-producing regions and give us greater control over our own energy future. Additionally, by developing advanced energy storage and grid technologies, we would enhance the resilience of our energy infrastructure, making it less vulnerable to cyberattacks or other threats.

Furthermore, D.S.I.R. would allow us to maintain our leadership in global energy markets. By exporting renewable energy technologies and expertise, we could compete with BRICS nations on the global stage and ensure that America remains the world's top energy innovator. This would not only enhance our economic influence but also strengthen our diplomatic and strategic relationships with other nations.

Legacy and Leadership

Mr. Trump, D.S.I.R. isn't just a plan for your second term—it's a legacy-defining initiative. Under your leadership, D.S.I.R. could transform America into a nation that leads the world in innovation, technology, and sustainability. It would cement your legacy as the president who not only restored America's greatness but also secured its future for generations to come.

Through your partnership with Elon Musk and the strategic guidance of Shango D'Allen, D.S.I.R. would create millions of jobs, modernize our infrastructure, and transition America to a clean energy future. It would position the U.S. as a global leader in renewable energy and innovation while countering the rising influence of BRICS.

The time to act is now. With D.S.I.R., you have the opportunity to not only win a second term but also leave an indelible mark on history. This plan addresses the most pressing issues of our time: economic instability, environmental degradation, and the growing threat from foreign adversaries. By acting decisively, you can steer America toward a future of prosperity, security, and sustainability.

Conclusion: A Bold Vision for America's Future

D.S.I.R. is more than just a policy initiative—it's a bold, transformative vision for America's future. A future where the U.S. leads the world in economic growth, technological innovation, and environmental stewardship. A future where millions of Americans are employed in high-quality, future-proof jobs, and where our roads, cities, and energy systems are powered by clean, renewable energy.

This is the future that D'Allen's Security, Infrastructure, and Renewable Energy Initiative offers. It's a future where the U.S. dollar is backed by energy reserves, ensuring its stability and dominance in the global economy. It's a future where America's infrastructure is modernized, making us a leader in electric vehicles, smart roads, and renewable energy technologies. And it's a future where America's energy independence and national security are assured through strategic investments in renewable energy and advanced infrastructure.

With Elon Musk by your side and the strategic vision of Shango D'Allen, you can make this future a reality, Mr. President. Together, you can lead America into a new era of prosperity, security, and sustainability—one where our best days are still ahead.

The world is watching, and the opportunity is now in your hands.

Chapter Twelve: Stimulate America's Future Tour (S.A.F.T.) and the Path Forward

Stimulate America's Future Tour (S.A.F.T.) is my life's work. It's a vision that I've spent over 30 years developing, evolving, and refining. The roots of S.A.F.T. run deep—deeper than any political campaign or fleeting initiative. It's not just a job creation program; it's a movement designed to tackle the core issues of economic inequality, joblessness, and the lack of opportunity in America's undeserved communities. It's an initiative born from decades of research, hands-on experience, and a deep desire to make a lasting difference in this country.

The Birth of a Vision

When I first began formulating the ideas behind S.A.F.T., the country was already showing signs of economic disparity that we see at an even larger scale today. Middle-class families were struggling to maintain their quality of life, manufacturing jobs were disappearing, and communities were being left behind as industries moved overseas. It was during these early years of witnessing these changes that I understood how deeply structural inequality runs in America. I saw how families were working two or three jobs just to make ends meet. I saw how children in low-income neighborhoods lacked access to quality education, job training, or even the basic resources they needed to thrive.

I knew something had to be done, but it couldn't be just another short-term, Band-Aid solution. It had to be transformative. It had to address the core issues that hold people back from reaching their full potential. And it had to be scalable— something that could be implemented in communities across the country, not just in isolated pockets.

Thus, the foundation of S.A.F.T. was laid. Over time, I gathered insights from entrepreneurs, educators, community leaders, and everyday working people. I sought out those who had overcome adversity to build their own path to success and asked them what resources would have made their journey easier. The answers varied, but one thing was always clear: people wanted real opportunities. They didn't want handouts; they wanted a pathway to success—something tangible that they could work toward.

A Holistic Approach to Empowerment

At its core, S.A.F.T. is built on the belief that economic empowerment must be comprehensive. It's not just about job creation, although that's a major part of it. It's about ensuring that people have the tools, education, and resources they need to build sustainable, long-term wealth and stability. It's about rebuilding our communities from the ground up—creating a ripple effect of prosperity that extends beyond just jobs and into the very fabric of our society.

S.A.F.T. focuses on several key pillars:

1. **Job Creation and Training**: The backbone of S.A.F.T. is creating 5 to 15 million new jobs across a range of industries, including renewable energy, construction, technology, and national security. These jobs won't be short-term, temporary positions; they will be long-term, sustainable careers that offer opportunities for advancement. Through a series of training programs, S.A.F.T. will ensure that people have the skills they need to succeed in these industries.

2. **Financial Literacy**: Job creation alone isn't enough. We also need to ensure that people understand how to manage their finances, invest in their future, and build wealth. S.A.F.T. will offer financial literacy programs that teach people how to budget, save, invest, and plan for retirement. This knowledge is essential for long-term economic stability.

3. **Infrastructure Renewal**: One of the biggest challenges facing America today is the state of our infrastructure. From crumbling roads and bridges to outdated energy grids, our country is in desperate need of modernization. S.A.F.T. will

work hand-in-hand with infrastructure projects like D.S.I.R. (D'Allen's Security, Infrastructure, and Renewable Energy Initiative) to ensure that communities across the country benefit from these improvements. By investing in infrastructure, we create jobs, improve quality of life, and position the U.S. as a leader in innovation and technology.

4. **Community Engagement**: S.A.F.T. isn't just about creating jobs and building infrastructure. It's about empowering communities to take control of their future. Through community engagement initiatives, S.A.F.T. will help local leaders, entrepreneurs, and residents come together to identify the unique challenges and opportunities in their area. By fostering collaboration, we can ensure that the benefits of S.A.F.T. are felt across all communities, not just a select few.

The S.A.F.T. Tour: Reaching Every Corner of America

S.A.F.T. will kick off with a nationwide tour, hitting 26 major U.S. cities across various regions. These live events will serve as the launchpad for the initiative, allowing us to connect directly with the people who will benefit from it the most. The S.A.F.T. tour will not just be job fairs or training sessions; they will be immersive experiences that bring together local governments, businesses, schools, and community organizations.

The tour will feature job creation opportunities, on-site training programs, workshops on financial literacy, and sessions where people can learn about infrastructure projects happening in their region. But the S.A.F.T. tour isn't just about providing information—it's about empowering people to take action. Attendees will walk away with concrete steps they can take to secure a job, improve their skills, or start their own business.

More importantly, the tour will foster a sense of community and shared purpose. When people see that there are tangible opportunities available in their own communities—when they see the investments being made in their future—it creates hope. It restores faith in the American Dream. It tells people, "You matter, and your future matters."

Revitalizing America's Workforce

One of the primary goals of S.A.F.T. is to revitalize America's workforce by creating jobs in industries that are poised for growth. Renewable energy, for example, is one of the fastest-growing sectors in the world. By investing in solar, wind, and other green energy initiatives, we can create millions of jobs while also addressing the urgent need to transition to cleaner energy sources.

But renewable energy is just one piece of the puzzle. S.A.F.T. will also focus on job creation in technology, cybersecurity, manufacturing, and national security. These industries offer long-term stability and growth potential, ensuring that the jobs created through S.A.F.T. are future-proof.

Through partnerships with educational institutions and private companies, S.A.F.T. will offer training programs that prepare workers for the jobs of tomorrow. Whether it's learning to build solar panels, install EV charging stations, or work in cybersecurity, S.A.F.T. will provide the training and resources people need to succeed in these new industries.

The Role of Financial Literacy

Creating jobs is essential, but it's not enough. If we want to ensure long-term economic stability for American families, we need to provide them with the tools to manage their finances wisely. That's why financial literacy is a core component of S.A.F.T.

Too often, people are trapped in a cycle of debt and financial insecurity because they don't have access to the education and resources they need to make informed financial decisions. S.A.F.T. will offer workshops and courses on topics like budgeting, saving, investing, and retirement planning. These programs will empower people to take control of their financial future and build generational wealth.

Moreover, S.A.F.T. will focus on undeserved communities where access to financial resources has historically been limited. By providing these communities with the knowledge and tools they need to manage their money effectively, we can help break the cycle of poverty and create lasting economic empowerment.

The Partnership with D.S.I.R.: A Perfect Match

While S.A.F.T. focuses on job creation, financial literacy, and community engagement, D.S.I.R. provides the large-scale infrastructure and energy projects that will drive economic growth for decades to come. Together, these two initiatives form a comprehensive strategy to rebuild America's economy, modernize our infrastructure, and secure our energy future.

By partnering with D.S.I.R., S.A.F.T. can ensure that the jobs being created through infrastructure projects are accessible to the communities that need them the most. Whether it's building roads, installing solar panels, or upgrading our energy grids, S.A.F.T. will provide the training and resources necessary to ensure that local residents are ready to take on these jobs.

Moreover, the partnership between S.A.F.T. and D.S.I.R. allows us to tackle multiple challenges at once. As we invest in renewable energy and infrastructure, we also create jobs, reduce carbon emissions, and strengthen our national security. It's a win-win for everyone involved.

The Power of Community Engagement

One of the most important aspects of S.A.F.T. is its focus on community engagement. Too often, large-scale initiatives are designed without input from the people they are meant to help. S.A.F.T. takes a different approach. By working directly with community leaders, local governments, and residents, we can ensure that the benefits of the initiative are felt across all communities.

Through town halls, focus groups, and community meetings, S.A.F.T. will listen to the unique needs and challenges of each region. This feedback will be used to tailor the initiative to the specific needs of each community, ensuring that S.A.F.T. delivers real, tangible benefits to the people who need them the most.

Moreover, by fostering a sense of ownership and involvement, S.A.F.T. will empower communities to take charge of their own future. When people are given the tools and resources to succeed, they are more likely to invest in their community, support local businesses, and work together to build a brighter future.

A Nationwide Impact: 26 Cities, Millions of Lives Changed

The S.A.F.T. tour will begin in 26 major U.S. cities, with plans to expand to even more communities across the country. These initial 26 cities have been chosen based on several factors: economic need, potential for infrastructure development, and historical underinvestment in job creation and educational resources. We are focusing on cities where the impact of S.A.F.T. will be felt the most, where communities are struggling with unemployment, lack of educational resources, and crumbling infrastructure. From the heart of the Rust Belt to the urban centers of the West Coast, S.A.F.T. is designed to bring opportunity to the places that need it most.

Each stop on the tour will be a multi-day event, bringing together local government officials, businesses, educators, and community leaders to discuss the unique challenges facing their region. These discussions will shape the next steps for S.A.F.T., ensuring that every city we visit sees real, tangible results that reflect the needs of the people. Our goal is to leave a lasting legacy in each city, not just in terms of job creation but in the form of educational programs, infrastructure projects, and community engagement initiatives that will continue long after the tour moves on.

A Personal Mission: The Evolution of S.A.F.T.

For me, S.A.F.T. isn't just a professional project; it's deeply personal. Having grown up in an environment where opportunities were limited, I've always understood the importance of giving people a chance to improve their lives. I've seen firsthand what happens when communities are left behind, and I've watched as promises made by politicians are rarely followed by action. That's why I'm so committed to making S.A.F.T. a reality, regardless of who holds office. This is a movement for the people—built by the people, for the people.

As a father and a grandfather, I've always thought about the world I want to leave behind for my children and grandchildren. S.A.F.T. represents my belief in the American Dream—a dream that is still alive, but one that needs real support to thrive in today's world. Too many families have been told that the American Dream is out of reach, that the opportunities once available to past generations no longer exist. But I refuse to accept that. I believe that with the right programs, the right leadership, and the right community engagement, we can bring back the American Dream and give every person the tools they need to succeed.

The Role of My Family: Legacy and Leadership

My family has been an integral part of this journey. They have inspired me, challenged me, and stood by me as I've worked tirelessly to build the foundation for S.A.F.T. Each of my children has played a role in shaping my understanding of what it means to create lasting change. They've given me insight into the next generation's hopes, fears, and dreams. As I've watched them grow, I've been even more motivated to ensure that S.A.F.T. provides opportunities not only for them but for their peers and the millions of young people across the country who deserve a chance to succeed.

My children, like many Americans, have had to navigate the challenges of a changing economy—an economy where traditional jobs are disappearing, where the cost of education is rising, and where financial security often feels elusive. Watching them carve their own paths has shown me the importance of adaptability, resilience, and perseverance. These are the values that S.A.F.T. is built on: the idea that with the right support, anyone can overcome adversity and build a brighter future.

As a father, I've also learned the importance of leadership by example. My children have seen firsthand the work I've put into S.A.F.T., and I hope that my dedication to this cause has inspired them to pursue their own dreams with the same passion and determination. I want to leave behind a legacy of hard work, integrity, and a commitment to helping others. S.A.F.T. is not just a program for me; it's part of my family's legacy—a legacy of giving back, of lifting others up, and of believing that everyone deserves a chance to succeed.

Why the Critics Have It Wrong: S.A.F.T. Is for Everyone

There will always be critics, and I expect no less with S.A.F.T. Some will argue that this is just another government program, another top-down initiative that won't actually solve the real problems facing the country. But they couldn't be more wrong. S.A.F.T. is different because it's built from the ground up. It's not about imposing a one-size-fits-all solution on every community. It's about listening to people, understanding their unique challenges, and providing them with the tools and resources they need to build their own path forward.

Critics might say that this type of initiative is too ambitious, that creating millions of jobs and revitalizing our infrastructure is an impossible task. But to those critics, I say: Look at history. America has always been a country that achieves the impossible. From the moon landing to the technological revolution, we've always been at our best when we set bold, ambitious goals and refuse to back down in the face of adversity.

S.A.F.T. is no different. Yes, it's ambitious. Yes, it's going to take time, effort, and resources to achieve. But it's also necessary. The problems we're facing as a country—rising economic inequality, crumbling infrastructure, and a lack of opportunity—won't be solved by small, incremental changes. They require bold action, and that's exactly what S.A.F.T. is designed to provide.

S.A.F.T. in Action: Real Stories, Real Impact

One of the most powerful aspects of S.A.F.T. is the real, tangible impact it will have on individuals and communities across the country. Let me share with you a few examples of how S.A.F.T. will transform lives.

Take, for example, a young man named Marcus in Detroit. Marcus grew up in a neighborhood that had been hit hard by the decline of the auto industry. Jobs were scarce, and opportunities were few. By the time he graduated high school, Marcus felt like his future was already set in stone: a series of dead-end jobs with no real prospects for advancement. But when the S.A.F.T. tour came to his city, everything changed.

Through the job training programs offered by S.A.F.T., Marcus was able to learn new skills in solar panel installation—a growing industry with plenty of job opportunities. Not only did Marcus land a job with a local company, but he also received ongoing support through S.A.F.T.'s financial literacy programs, helping him manage his new income, save for the future, and even start investing. Today, Marcus is not only employed, but he's also helping to train others in his community, creating a ripple effect of opportunity and growth.

Then there's Maria, a single mother in Houston. For years, Maria struggled to make ends meet, working multiple jobs just to keep food on the table for her two children. She had dreams of starting her own business but lacked the resources and connections to make it a reality. When S.A.F.T. arrived in her city, she attended one of the small business workshops and connected with mentors who helped her develop a business plan and secure a small loan to get started.

With the support of S.A.F.T., Maria was able to open her own food truck, specializing in authentic, homemade Mexican cuisine. Not only is her business thriving, but she's also been able to hire other single mothers in her community, providing them with jobs and a sense of purpose. S.A.F.T. didn't just change Maria's life—it transformed the lives of her children and her entire community.

The Path Forward: What's Next for S.A.F.T.

As we look ahead to the future, the path forward for S.A.F.T. is clear: expand, adapt, and continue to listen to the needs of the people. The 26-city tour is just the beginning. Over the next decade, we aim to reach every corner of the United States, ensuring that no community is left behind. We will continue to partner with local governments, businesses, and educational institutions to ensure that the resources provided by S.A.F.T. are tailored to the unique needs of each region.

But S.A.F.T. isn't just about America's present—it's about our future. We must think long-term, considering not only the immediate impact of job creation and infrastructure development but also the future of work in a rapidly changing economy. Automation, artificial intelligence, and climate change will all play a role in shaping the jobs of tomorrow, and S.A.F.T. is prepared to meet these challenges head-on.

We will continue to invest in industries that are poised for growth, ensuring that American workers have the skills they need to compete in the global economy. Whether it's renewable energy, advanced manufacturing, or cutting-edge technology, S.A.F.T. will provide the training and resources necessary to prepare our workforce for the jobs of the future.

A Call to Action: Join the Movement

S.A.F.T. isn't just my vision—it's a movement that belongs to all of us. Whether you're a business owner, an educator, a community leader, or an everyday working person, there's a role for you in this movement. The problems we're facing as a nation are too big for any one person or organization to solve alone. We need all hands on deck.

So, I'm calling on you to join the S.A.F.T. movement. Attend a tour event in your city, sign up for one of our training programs, or volunteer your time and expertise to help those in your community. Together, we can create a future where every American has the opportunity to succeed, thrive, and build a better life for themselves and their families.

The time for change is now. The path forward is clear. Let's work together to build the future that we all deserve—a future where opportunity, prosperity, and hope are available to everyone.

Chapter Thirteen: Final Thoughts: More Than Just a Vision

As we bring this journey to a close, let me be clear from the outset: this book wasn't written simply to express opinions. It's more than that. This book is a blueprint, a roadmap, a call to action for anyone who cares about the future of America. It's not just about politics—it's about you, your family, your community, and how we can all work together to rebuild this country in ways that make it stronger, more prosperous, and more united than it's ever been.

Over the course of the past 11 chapters, I've shared my vision for how we can address some of the most pressing issues facing our nation—whether it's economic instability, healthcare, education, immigration, or crime. These are not abstract, theoretical problems; they're the real, tangible challenges that millions of Americans face every day. And if you've stayed with me through all of this, I know that you're here because you want change just as much as I do. You care about the future of this country, and you're ready to take action.

This isn't the end of a conversation—it's the beginning. The future is ours to shape, and I believe we can make America not just great again, but greater than it's ever been.

The Economy: A New Beginning

We started this journey by tackling the heart of American life: the economy. Every American feels the weight of a broken system where wages don't keep up with the cost of living, where taxes are too high, and where small businesses—the backbone of our economy—are stifled by endless regulations. People are not just struggling; they're suffocating.

The American Dream feels further away than ever for many families, and that's unacceptable.

The solution isn't a band-aid fix. It's not about minor tweaks or incremental changes. It's about a complete reset, a full-scale transformation of how we approach economic policy in this country. That's why I've proposed a 75% tax cut for five years. Yes, you read that right—a dramatic, bold move that will allow people to rebuild their lives, reinvest in their futures, and breathe again. It's time to stop nickel-and-diming people with high taxes while throwing them crumbs in return.

This is where D.S.I.R. (D'Allen's Security, Infrastructure, and Renewable Energy Initiative) comes in. It's a comprehensive plan designed to overhaul our economic, infrastructure, and energy systems. And while I've put forward Donald Trump as the leader best equipped to implement such a plan, let's be clear: this idea isn't tied to any one politician. It's bigger than that. It's about the future of America, and D.S.I.R. is the kind of bold strategy we need to regain economic strength, create millions of jobs, and secure long-term prosperity.

But even if Trump or another leader doesn't adopt this plan, that's where S.A.F.T. (Stimulate America's Future Tour) comes in. S.A.F.T. isn't just a policy initiative—it's a grassroots movement. It's about engaging millions of people across the country, connecting them to real opportunities—jobs, training programs, and resources—that will enable them to thrive. S.A.F.T. will launch regardless of who holds political power, because at its core, it's a movement driven by the people, for the people. And it's been 30 years in the making.

Healthcare: Taking on Corporate Greed

The healthcare system in this country is broken, and everyone knows it. The reason for this? Corporate greed. The insurance companies and pharmaceutical giants have turned healthcare into a profit machine, and they've been allowed to do so by a government that's too cozy with these industries. It's time to stop pretending that this system is working for anyone other than the people at the top.

What did I propose? A bold, disruptive idea—let the government get into the health business, not to control it but to create competition. Just like T-Mobile shook up the cellphone industry by offering better deals and forcing other companies to lower their prices, the government can do the same in healthcare. We can't continue to let insurance and pharmaceutical companies dictate the cost of care while millions of Americans are left struggling to afford basic medical services.

This doesn't mean abandoning capitalism. On the contrary, a healthy capitalist system thrives on competition. What we have now is a system where a handful of companies control everything and exploit the very people they're supposed to serve. It's time to put an end to that and focus on making healthcare affordable, accessible, and focused on what matters most—patient care, not profits.

Immigration: Securing Our Borders and Our Future

The border crisis isn't just a failure of policy—it's a failure of leadership. And let's be clear: this isn't about opposing immigration. I've said it before, and I'll say it again—I'm pro-legal immigration. This country was built by immigrants, and that's one of our greatest strengths. But what we're seeing now with the flood of illegal immigration, combined with the influx of drugs and crime, is unsustainable and dangerous.

We need to seal the border, full stop. That's the only way we can protect our citizens, our values, and our way of life. But that doesn't mean closing the door on legal immigrants who want to come to this country to build a better life. We need a system that works, one that honors the rule of law and provides opportunities for those who come here legally and respect the process.

The truth is, many of the policies being pushed by Democrats around immigration feel like part of a broader, strategic agenda—one that's designed to secure political power by shifting the demographic balance in their favor. But this short-term political gain comes at the expense of national security and the well-being of American citizens.

Crime: Reform, Don't Abandon

The debate around policing in America has been one of the most polarizing topics of recent years. The calls to "defund the police" that erupted after high-profile cases of police brutality missed the mark. We don't need to abandon law enforcement—we need to reform it. That's a key distinction that often gets lost in the noise.

As I mentioned in earlier chapters, I've had personal experiences with both sides of this issue. I've encountered corrupt police officers who abused their power, and I've also met officers who truly care about the communities they serve and want to make a positive difference. We can't throw the baby out with the bathwater.

What we need is better training, stricter accountability, and stronger relationships between law enforcement and the communities they protect. The Democratic Party, the same party that pushed for the 1994 Crime Bill that led to mass incarceration, is now pushing to defund the police. It's hypocrisy at its finest.

We need law and order in this country, but it has to be law and order that works for everyone. Reform is necessary, but dismantling the entire system is not the answer.

Education: Preparing the Next Generation

Our education system is broken—there's no other way to put it. Our children are being taught to conform to outdated systems that don't prepare them for the challenges of the modern world. They're not being taught how to succeed in life; they're being taught how to survive in a system that's set up to benefit a select few.

What do we need? Longer school years, yes—but more importantly, we need better schools. We need to focus on teaching our kids the skills they'll need to thrive in the 21st century. That means teaching them about investments, financial management, entrepreneurship, and community building. It means teaching them how to lead, not just follow.

Through S.A.F.T. and D.S.I.R., we have the opportunity to not only rebuild our infrastructure but also to reshape our education system. If we're preparing our country for the future, why not prepare our children to be the ones who will manage and grow that future? Let's give them the tools to succeed, not just as workers but as leaders, innovators, and changemakers.

Social Security: A Broken System in Need of Reform

When I think about Social Security, I'm reminded of the advice my father and uncle gave me when I was young: "Take care of your old man." It's advice that took me years to fully understand. They weren't just talking about taking care of them—they were talking about taking care of ourselves, making sure that we had the financial security to support our families and our communities as we grew older.

But the Social Security system we have today is failing. It's not enough to support the millions of Americans who depend on it, and it's only going to get worse as more and more people retire. We need to rethink Social Security, not just as a government program but as part of a broader strategy to ensure financial security for all Americans.

Through S.A.F.T., I've developed a plan to help those who are often forgotten—seniors, veterans, the homeless, and orphans. These are the people who need our help the most, and we can't afford to wait for the government to fix it. It's up to us to step up and take action.

Abortion: Beyond the Political Rhetoric

The abortion debate in this country is far more complex than most people realize. Too many of us are quick to jump into the argument without fully understanding the legal and moral implications. Whether it's Roe v. Wade or Dobbs v. Jackson Women's Health Organization, people are making decisions based on headlines, not facts.

Let me be clear: I believe in a woman's right to choose, but I also believe in personal responsibility and informed decision-making. This isn't about taking away rights; it's about ensuring that people understand the full weight of the choices they're making. We're in a society that often values convenience over consequence, and that has led to a lot of confusion and misinformation surrounding the issue of abortion.

Roe v. Wade didn't make abortion a free-for-all, and Dobbs v. Jackson didn't criminalize it across the board. What these rulings did was allow states to determine their own policies regarding abortion, which is where the debate needs to be focused now—at the state level. People need to educate themselves about the laws in their own states and take action accordingly. Don't let politicians manipulate you into believing that every change is an attack on women's rights. Understand the nuances, and make decisions that align with your values.

To Black and Brown women, especially, I urge you to be cautious of the narratives being sold to you. Too often, we are manipulated into thinking that certain politicians are on our side when, in reality, they are using us for votes without delivering meaningful changes in our lives. Protect your autonomy, but also make sure that you're informed about the larger forces at play. Don't let anyone use your body or your voice as a pawn in a political game.

At the end of the day, abortion is a deeply personal issue, and it should be treated as such. The conversation should be led by women—not men, not politicians, and certainly not corporations. Women should have the space to discuss, debate, and decide on this issue without external pressures clouding their judgment. But this conversation should also involve education and personal accountability. We must take a balanced approach, one that considers the moral, legal, and personal dimensions of the issue. It's not black and white, and we shouldn't pretend that it is.

The Future: It's In Our Hands

As I wrap up this book, I want to emphasize one thing: the future of America is in our hands. We can't afford to sit back and wait for politicians to fix things for us, because they won't. We've seen time and time again that the people in power often don't have our best interests at heart. Whether it's the economy, healthcare, immigration, crime, education, or any of the other critical issues we've discussed, the solutions won't come from the top down. They will come from us.

That's why S.A.F.T. is so important. It's more than a plan or an initiative—it's a movement. It's a way for people from all walks of life to come together and take control of their own destinies. Whether it's through job creation, financial literacy, infrastructure development, or community engage-ment, S.A.F.T. provides the tools and resources needed to build a better future for all Americans.

This isn't just about providing opportunities for individuals— it's about transforming entire communities. It's about restoring hope in places where hope has been lost. It's about giving people the power to rebuild their lives, their neighborhoods, and their country. S.A.F.T. isn't just my vision; it's our vision. It's a vision of an America that works for everyone, not just the privileged few.

And let's not forget the role that D.S.I.R. (D'Allen's Security, Infrastructure, and Renewable Energy Initiative) plays in this vision. Together, S.A.F.T. and D.S.I.R. form a comprehensive strategy to address the most critical challenges facing our nation. From economic revitalization to energy independence, these initiatives offer real solutions to the problems that have plagued us for far too long.

The Role of Leadership: Trump and Beyond

I've been vocal about my support for Donald Trump and his potential role in adopting the D.S.I.R. strategy. I believe that under his leadership, we can see bold, transformative changes that other politicians are too afraid to tackle. Trump has the ability to think outside the box and take decisive action, and that's exactly what this country needs right now.

But I want to be clear: this isn't about Trump. It's about leadership. Whether it's Trump or someone else, we need leaders who are willing to take risks, challenge the status quo, and put the needs of the American people first. We need leaders who understand that the problems we face require bold solutions, not just empty promises.

S.A.F.T. and D.S.I.R. aren't tied to any one politician. They're tied to a vision for America's future—one that's built on innovation, resilience, and a commitment to creating real opportunities for all. Whether Trump is in office or not, these initiatives will move forward because they're rooted in the needs of the people, not the whims of politicians.

A Call to Action: Your Role in America's Future

Now that we've reached the end of this journey, I'm going to ask something of you. I'm going to ask you to get involved.

I didn't write this book just to share my thoughts. I wrote it to spark action. I wrote it to inspire you to take the next step—whether that means joining the S.A.F.T. movement, engaging in local politics, or simply starting a conversation with your neighbors about the issues that matter most. Every single one of us has a role to play in building the future of this country.

America wasn't built by spectators—it was built by doers. By people who saw a problem and decided to take action. By people who refused to accept the status quo and worked tirelessly to create something better. That's what this country was founded on, and that's what we need to get back to.

So, I'm asking you: What will your role be? Will you sit on the sidelines, or will you get in the game? Will you watch as others try to fix the problems, or will you step up and take part in the solution? The choice is yours.

The Legacy We Leave Behind

I'm not just thinking about today—I'm thinking about the future. I'm thinking about the world we'll leave behind for our children and grandchildren. I'm thinking about the legacy that we, as a generation, will leave behind.

Will it be a legacy of division, stagnation, and missed opportunities? Or will it be a legacy of growth, innovation, and progress?

Through S.A.F.T. and D.S.I.R., we have the chance to leave behind a legacy of real, lasting change. We have the chance to rebuild America from the ground up, creating a country where every person has the opportunity to succeed, where communities are strong and thriving, and where the American Dream is not just an ideal but a reality for all.

This is more than just a vision—it's a mission. And I'm asking you to join me on this journey.

Moving Forward Together

This book may be coming to an end, but the work is just beginning. Together, we can transform this country. Together, we can address the challenges that have held us back for too long. Together, we can build an America that is stronger, fairer, and more united than ever before.

I want to thank you for taking the time to read this book and for being part of this journey. But more importantly, I want to thank you for caring about the future of America. Because it's people like you—people who care, people who are willing to take action—that will make all the difference.

So let's move forward together. Let's take the ideas and strategies we've discussed here and turn them into action. Let's build a future that we can all be proud of—a future where every American has the opportunity to succeed, where our communities are thriving, and where our country is stronger than ever.

The future is in our hands. Let's get to work.

— -

About the Author

About the Author: A Journey of Resilience, Responsibility, and Service

Shango D'Allen was born in 1973 at Beth Israel Hospital in Boston, Massachusetts. His early life was shaped by an overwhelming sense of independence, as he found himself responsible for his own well-being at the tender age of 11. Although he was not technically an orphan, his circumstances made him feel as though he were, navigating the world without the safety net of constant parental support. Each passing year demanded more maturity, more responsibility, and more self-reliance from him. But despite these challenges, one constant remained: his deep admiration and love for his father, who he always considered his hero.

His father, a man of great wisdom and resilience, shaped many of Shango's values and life philosophies. Though the relationship between them was profound, Shango wrestled with feelings of abandonment from others who were supposed to be there for him. These emotional scars left a lasting impact, fueling his drive to make a better life for himself and those around him. His father's influence guided him through the storm of adolescence, and the lessons he learned about responsibility, hard work, and self-reliance stuck with him as he became the man he is today.

Music played an enormous role in helping Shango cope with the emotional turmoil of his early life. Across a variety of genres, he found solace and inspiration, developing a deep love for music that transcended all boundaries—except for new-school country. His favorite five songs are a reflection of his life journey, full of passion, struggle, and perseverance: Lenny Williams' "Cause I Love You," Slash's "Obsession Confession," Tupac's "I Ain't Mad at Cha," Silk's "Lose Control," and Eminem's "Lose Yourself." Each of these songs holds deep meaning for Shango, representing the different stages of his emotional evolution and his continued determination to rise above the challenges life has thrown his way.

Beyond music, Shango's passions are as diverse and adventurous as the life he's led. Whether cliff diving into deep waters, jet skiing at breakneck speeds, or camping in the wilderness, Shango finds peace in the beauty of nature and the thrill of pushing himself beyond his limits. Four-wheeling and white-water rafting give him an outlet for the boundless energy he channels into his life, while his love for finding beautiful, secluded spots with outdoor bathtubs provides him with moments of quiet reflection. These are the times when

Shango connects most deeply with his inner self and his purpose, often accompanied by someone special who shares in the beauty of these experiences.

Shango's competitive nature is perhaps best exemplified in his love for basketball. His top five players—Kareem Abdul-Jabbar, Michael Jordan, Shaquille O'Neal, Kobe Bryant, and Larry Bird—represent the perfect combination of talent, perseverance, and the relentless drive for greatness. Each of these athletes reflects a quality Shango holds dear: the desire to excel, the commitment to hard work, and the determination to be the best version of oneself.

But above all, Shango's greatest passion is for the people he cares about. He prides himself on being the go-to person for his family and friends when they need support, advice, or someone to give them tough love. Whether it's offering optimistic guidance, crafting logical solutions to complex problems, or giving someone a much-needed push to face their own fears, Shango is always there—steadfast, caring, and honest. He doesn't shy away from hard conversations, but he always approaches them with the intention of building others up, never tearing them down.

Looking toward the future, Shango has a clear vision for the remainder of his life: service. After years of building himself up and overcoming his own struggles, he now dedicates himself to uplifting others. His mission is to serve those who are often overlooked by society: the elderly, orphans, veterans, the homeless, the hungry, and those who have lost their way. Shango is driven by the belief that to secure his place in the afterlife, he must do far more good than bad in this world. Reflecting on his youthful mistakes, Shango feels a deep responsibility to make amends by doing as much good as possible for those who need it most.

This belief has shaped the core of his life's mission and the ideas outlined in his book. His vision isn't just a collection of theoretical solutions to society's problems—it's a practical, actionable plan that he has spent decades developing. Shango's goal is to create tangible, positive change in the world, starting with the people who are most vulnerable. He believes that by uplifting the marginalized and giving them the tools they need to succeed, we can all build a better, more compassionate society together.

Shango's ideas don't just stem from a desire to fix what's broken in society—they come from a place of deep love and respect for humanity. He knows that real change starts with understanding and empathy, and his life's work is dedicated to embodying those qualities. In every interaction, every project, and every initiative he undertakes, Shango seeks to make the world a better place for those who need it most. He's not content to stand by and watch while others suffer—he's committed to being an active participant in the process of healing and growth, both for individuals and society as a whole.

His book reflects this commitment to action. It's not just a manifesto—it's a blueprint for how we can all take part in the transformation of our country. Shango challenges his readers to join him in this mission, to be more than spectators in the fight for a better world. He believes that together, we can create lasting change by focusing on the things that matter most: economic stability, community support, and a renewed sense of purpose for every American.

As you've read throughout this book, Shango has big ideas. His plans, such as D.S.I.R. (D'Allen's Security, Infrastructure, and Renewable Energy Initiative) and S.A.F.T. (Stimulate America's Future Tour), are ambitious in scope and transformative in their potential. He believes that with the right leadership—particularly under a re-elected Donald Trump—these plans can be realized on a national scale, helping millions of Americans find stability, opportunity, and hope for the future.

But even if these ideas don't catch the attention of politicians or leaders, Shango is determined to press on. He's not waiting for permission to make a difference—he's already working on it. Whether through his personal efforts or the broader initiatives he champions, Shango is dedicated to creating a world where every person has the opportunity to succeed.

At the core of everything he does is a simple but powerful belief: to make it to heaven, you must do more good than bad. Shango doesn't know exactly where the scales lie in his own life, but he's not taking any chances. He's determined to tip the balance in favor of good by dedicating his life to service, compassion, and the pursuit of justice for all.

For Shango D'Allen, life is not just about surviving—it's about thriving, and helping others to do the same. Every chapter of his life has been a testament to the power of resilience, self-determination, and the willingness to fight for what you believe in. Now, as he embarks on the next phase of his journey, he invites you to join him in this mission. Together, we can build a brighter, more just world where everyone has the opportunity to fulfill their potential.

Respectfully submitted,

D'Allen Family, LLC

dallenfamilyllc@gmail.com

trumphasmyvoteperiod2024@gmail.com

trumphasmyvoteperiod.com